From Middle England

By the same Author

From Middle England

a memory of the 1930s

PHILIP OAKES

ANDRE DEUTSCH

First published 1980 by
André Deutsch Limited
105 Great Russell Street London WC1

Printed in Great Britain by
Lowe & Brydone Printers Limited
Thetford Norfolk

ISBN 0 233 97232 3

For my children

One

I ALWAYS had difficulty in putting on my cravat, especially on the morning the school broke up for the summer holidays. The cravat was made up of three linen flaps, sewn together like pages in a rag book, the edges starched to a razor sharpness. The first flap slotted behind my collar band, nicking my throat when I turned my head. The middle flap was impaled on the top button of my blue serge cloak. The last one hung free, clanking faintly against my chest. End of term made my hands shake with excitement. Sweat dewed my fingers, soiling the fabric. The button fought the buttonhole. Sometimes the rigid linen drew blood, as if tracing a line for the headsman's axe. The cloak had eight silver buttons embossed with the initials of the school. Around my waist I wore a narrow black belt. My trousers were short, made of black moleskin, stiff enough to stand up by themselves. 'I think you look very smart' said my mother, proud of the uniform, proud that I was a Blue-coat boy. No one else in my family had been to a public school. My passing discomfort was a small price to pay for the privilege.

The school was in Wolverhampton, a few miles out of the town, lying back from the road, drenched in Virginia creeper, its clock tower separating the boys' and girls' wings. It had been founded in 1850 by a tradesman named John Lees, whose ghost, riding on the back of a Great Dane, was reputed to haunt the main dormitory. Sometimes I woke, between midnight and dawn, the night-lights burning dimly in the vaulted roof, and imagined him padding by. Small sausages of wool and dust blown by the draught that seeped through the windows kept open all year round, rolled silently beneath the beds. I drew my knees to my chest and tucked my feet under the hem of my nightshirt. I could hear the tick of the hound's nails on the waxed floor. I could feel the dead eyes of Mr Lees boring through my scarlet blanket. I whimpered with fright. The need to relieve myself became urgent, but the lavatory was at the distant end of the dormitory, a hundred miles away and infested by other phantoms. I said the Lord's Prayer, adding as a postscript a full confession of my sins – cribbing in maths, hoarding bubblegum, drawing a naked lady in the back of my prayer book. The hound sauntered on to haunt another dreamer and gradually I lowered myself back into sleep, drawing it over my head like the lips of a sack, until the bell rang at seven and I woke again to face another day.

I was enrolled as a pupil at the school in 1936 when I was eight years old. My father had died four years previously and my mother was an invalid. She had been a teacher, a profession to which she had returned after my father's death, but one day she collapsed in the street, almost falling through the plate-glass window of Woolworth's and after months of examinations and consultations a tumour was discovered on the right-hand side of her brain. It was removed by a surgeon ('pioneer surgery' said my Aunt Ada as if, in some way, the family had contributed to science) and, although her life was saved, her left arm and leg were strangely insensitive. She stumbled and dropped things. Cups and saucers shattered on the red and black tiles of the kitchen floor. Several times when she was poking the fire she fell into it. The paralysis – for so she learned to call it – became worse and for much of the time she was bed-ridden. Home was no place for me to be.

While she was in the nursing home I stayed with my step-brother and his wife Rooney, a cross and baby-faced woman who earned my puzzled enmity by reminding me that, because my mother paid nothing for my support, I was not entitled to share the chocolates which she popped into the mouth of her younger son.

'I don't want any chocolates,' I said.

She smiled and licked her fingers. 'That's all right then. There won't be many chocolates where you're going.'

'What do you mean?'

'You're going away to boarding school,' she said. 'Somewhere grand, they tell me.'

'Like Greyfriars?' I asked, quite unalarmed. I had recently started to read *The Magnet* magazine and my notions of public school were pleasantly coloured by the stories of Harry Wharton and Co. It seemed a preferable life to that I shared unwillingly with Rooney and her family.

She stirred the chocolates with her forefinger and chose an almond cream. 'I don't know about Greyfriars,' she said, compressing her mouth into a soft beak as she sucked the cream from the chocolate shell. 'All I know is you wear funny clothes. It's called a Bluecoat school because you wear a blue cloak and yellow stockings.'

'Why?' I demanded.

'Because you're different,' said Rooney with well-judged malice. 'People who are different wear different clothes.'

She was wrong about the yellow stockings. They were the distinctive leg-wear of Christ's Hospital while ours were a nondescript grey. But the difference she imagined between Bluecoat boys and the rest of the school-going world was real enough. The uniform was picturesque and distinctive. It made old soldiers straighten their backs and their wives cry. But weeks later, when my mother showed me a photograph of a boy wearing it, my spirits drooped. It was like fancy dress. Studying the picture I imagined fingers pointing at me, eyes studying me over the tops of newspapers. It was an appalling prospect. I wished passionately not to be different, but the uniform promised to set me apart. Where the difference began was not important. The costume made it absolute.

'I don't want to go to that school,' I said. 'I want to stay with you.'

My mother shook her head. 'You can't. There's no one here to look after you. You can see that, surely. I'm laid up half the time and the house is like a hospital. It's not good for you. You should be with boys of your own age. And think of the education! It's a wonderful chance. Everyone's worked so hard to make it possible. You should be grateful.' She was crying. Tears were coursing down her face, but unmistakably she was angry too. What was happening was not her fault. She was acting in my best interests and I was making difficulties. What was worse, I was wilfully closing my eyes to a future denied to her but which, miraculously, beckoned me. I was committing a cardinal sin. I was refusing to better myself. I was rejecting an opportunity.

Even at the age of eight I knew the seriousness of my offence. Education raged through my mother's family like strong drink, the only intoxicant permitted by a brood of North Staffordshire Methodists whose philosophy of life was based on a set of gritty maxims in which Plain Living, High Thinking ran a close second to Waste Not, Want Not. My mother's name was Constance. She had thick black hair, a stubborn jaw and bright blue eyes and she was the youngest of nine children, loved and spoiled by her brothers and sisters John and Joe and Percy and Ernest and Frank and Anice and Ada and Jenny. Her mother tended house – a red brick back-to-back in Burslem – and her father made wooden crates in which ware left the pot-banks on barges which butted their way through the tawny network of canals veining England. It was a family in which nothing of value was achieved without effort and the effort came as naturally as breathing. Frank studied hard and became a civil engineer. Percy studied hard and became a teacher. My mother herself taught a class of thirty when she was only fifteen. The drive and the impulse were both irresistible and my feeble objection to going away to school was a kind of heresy.

'Mary could look after me,' I said.

My mother shook her head again. 'Mary has her hands full already. She has the shopping and the cooking and the cleaning. We've got the sweep coming next week, then the curtains to wash. She hasn't the time to look after you.'

'She wouldn't mind,' I said.

My mother clapped her hands sharply. 'That's enough,' she said. 'You're just being selfish. You're not part of Mary's job.'

Mary Evans was my mother's housekeeper. She came from the nearby mining village of Smallthorne; a short, squat woman who swaggered like a sailor on bandy legs and whose working dresses were stiff beneath the arms with dried sweat. Her hair was a sparse and silky bob, as golden as the nib of my fountain pen, and when she washed it she tucked it beneath a net which left her ears jutting out like pink and white lamb chops. The top joint was missing from the third finger of her right hand and when she was dusting or carrying coal she protected the stump with a stall of chamoix leather. She had cut the finger, she told me, when she was a girl and already keeping house for a miner and his three sons. There had been no time to let it heal, what with scrubbing floors and washing clothes, and the wound festered. 'Doctor sent me to the infirmary and they chopped it off,' she told me. My mother relished her stoicism and, in turn, was flattered by Mary's admiration of the family. Each supplied a need in the other and it was not for me to upset the balance.

It was, I realised, a delicate thing. We lived in an avenue of pebble-dashed semis whose windows and leaded lights turned hopefully towards green fields. Behind us on the other side of High Lane, which marked the top of the avenue like a sharply raised spine, lay the Potteries. Looking down from the ridge on a working day was like peering into a bowl of milk. Pot-banks and factories pumped out their pall of smoke and when the sun shone you could see the golden angel on the roof of Burslem's public library treading the haze, while beneath him the town drowned. There was no smoke on Sundays. The ovens were banked and it was as though a layer of soiled air had been peeled away to reveal streets, roof-tops, chapels and the meat market standing four square in sable granite. This was where my mother's family came from, the warmly remembered but outgrown past. The avenue stood for the future. Even after four years the estate had not been completed. Opposite our house was a patch we knew as The Waste. There were a few allotments strung round with split palings, a hen run and a corrugated shed. The rest was open land, pink with willow herb and bumpy with little hills of bald yellow clay. It was a safe playground, close to home but sufficiently private to light fires without being seen. Further afield was Banky Brook, a black oily stream running from Sneyd Green colliery, to be jumped at its widest part as an initiation rite, and a small marsh in which hundreds of frogs squatted, only the knobs of their eyes showing above the weeds. There were leeches writhing like black silk concertinas in the mud and minnows that somehow survived the brackish water. I caught them in a muslin net and kept them in a jam jar until, without warning or explanation, they died and floated belly up, their mouths framing a silent reproach.

Along the lane was Mary's village, Smallthorne, a place of fierce, black-faced men with livid eyeballs and lips like cherries. Between shifts at the pit they met at the bottom of the avenue, white silk chokers round their necks, whippets to heel. They raced pigeons, played pitch and toss and swore loudly and continuously. They also got drunk. To my mother, who was a strict teetotaller, this was not only disgusting but criminal. Times were hard, every penny mattered. It was wrong, she felt, to squander hard-earned money on beer. To point the lesson she would fill a glass with water and drain it in a gulp. 'Adam's grog,' she would say, smacking her lips and patting her stomach. It was a text which she used as the basis for many sermons.

She did not regard herself as a snob. She had nothing against the miners, but they represented the unregenerate side of the Potteries, a lawless breed who could be redeemed only with the help of God and education. She regarded them as a missionary would view a tribe of cannibals. If they were to be saved we first had to set an example. If fraternisation was necessary, it was to be endured but not necessarily enjoyed. My best friend at the Infant School was a miner's son named Gordon Parker. He lived in a narrow black house, cramped as a coffin, in a terrace row near the Palace Cinema, known to its patrons as 'the bug-hutch'.

Every morning at seven the doorstep was scrubbed and blancoed with yellow brick. The paintwork was chocolate brown and there were lace curtains at the windows. When I went home with him we passed through the back yard where ferrets blinked red eyes through the bars of their cages and into the kitchen where a huge fire licked the chimney back and washed the room to the colour of roses. A kettle steamed on the hob and there were steel engravings on the walls. Every surface danced with points of ruby light.

Miners, said my mother, were lucky enough to get free coal. It glowed in the grate like lava.

For hours we sat poring through piles of *Hotspurs* and *Wizards*. When it grew dark Gordon's mother lit the lamps. The wind sucked at the fire down the chimney and the gas jets sighed in their mantles. We ate broken bread, doused in hot milk and sprinkled with sugar. It was delicious. Later, when I described it to Mary Evans she pursed her lips in disapproval. 'Tha's been eating pobs,' she said. 'Baby's food. It's not for the likes of you.' When Gordon came to our house he was offered cucumber sandwiches and Rice Krispies. I waited for him to demand something more substantial, but I was disappointed. He emptied both plates and looked hopefully for more. It was, he told my mother, the best food he had ever tasted. Gordon was not a member of the avenue gang. No blackball was enforced, but he was not sufficiently local to be one of us. Living half a mile away put him into another territory. Like an animal he smelt differently, he observed different rituals, different customs. Our membership depended almost entirely on proximity. No more than a hundred yards separated any of our houses: it was as though an invisible network of paths joined door to door and like dogs or drunk men we knew them by instinct, selecting the route most appropriate to the time of day or the day of the week. Robbie Cook, who lived opposite, slept late. He was a tall, pale boy with liquid brown eyes and hair which his mother watered down each morning and combed into strands like splintered wood. He was always the last to have breakfast, sleepily spooning up his boiled egg and once, as if in a dream, dipping his finger in the yolk and drawing a tacky yellow badge on the breast of his jersey. I watched with bated breath, waiting for his mother to scold him. But instead she exploded into incredulous laughter, marvelling that her son should be so perverse and so original as to paint himself with an egg.

On either side of me lived Edwin Jones, whose mother was divorced, and Roy Greaves, whose father was a director of the local bus company. Roy's family was rich. They had a car in the garage and a cocktail cabinet which contained not only sherry and gin but, more exotically, a bottle of mysterious verdant fluid called 'Five O'Clock Cocktail'. Roy smuggled a measure out of the house in a medicine bottle and we drank it, sitting around a fire on The Waste. It tasted like cough mixture and when I spilled a drop on the embers at my feet, burst into a small but vivid fireball. It was a more effective demonstration of the perils of alcohol than all my mother's sermons. Roy was the only member of the gang who had seen a naked woman. When his grandmother died she was laid out in the front bedroom and Roy had crept in and lifted her nightgown. He could or would not describe clearly what he had seen, but his experience made him at once sinister and unique.

Edwin Jones was extraordinary only by proxy. His mother, having taken the name of her second husband, was Mrs Pointon. She had soon parted from him so that mother and son bearing different names lived in a house from which the man was absent. The arrangement was difficult to understand, but even harder was to try and imagine what had brought the Pointons together in the first place. He was a mild, reticent man who worked as a manager at Sneyd Colliery, while his wife seemed to be living out a private melodrama, full of deceits and betrayals, none of them made explicit but all darkly suggested by a broken phrase or a forlorn gesture. Her laugh was shrill, violent and sustained; a long rivet of sound. She would stand by the front gate, her arms tightly folded across her chest, her thin hair plucked by the wind, gazing tragically towards the distant colliery where Mr Pointon went about his business. On his visits to see his wife he would sometimes stop by to visit my mother. It was no more than a courtesy but Mrs Pointon seized on a different interpretation and, abruptly, the visits ceased. Passing our house he would slow down, smile nervously and raise his cap, then hurry on. He, too, seemed baffled by the turn his life had taken. Behind his steel-rimmed spectacles his eyes were watery and bemused.

John Whitcomb lived at the bottom of the avenue. His father was the head of a local secondary school, drawling and sardonic, with an acrid wit and a parched yellow face. His mother had a frizz of orange hair and wore large, perfectly round glasses like racing goggles. She was a chain smoker and I rarely saw her without a cigarette jammed in her bright red mouth. Ash freckled her chest and she coughed constantly, never removing the cigarette but wheezing around it like an engine erupting around the starting plug which kicked it into life. The year before my mother went into the nursing home John had an operation on his heart. That summer he spent every fine day on a camp bed in the garden with a pile of books and a wind-up gramophone within reach. Our favourite record was 'Tiger Rag' played by Harry Roy and his Band; on the reverse side was 'Bugle Call Rag'. I sat on the grass sipping Mrs Whitcomb's lemonade and watching cats stalk each other through the pink thickets of the rhubarb plantation. Planes from Meir aerodrome close to Hanley droned through the cloudless sky, banking over Smallthorne and sliding away behind the colliery tips that pricked the horizon like black pyramids. Flights in the plane cost five shillings a time. We all longed to take what we knowingly termed 'a quick flip', but our parents objected. Planes crashed, passengers died; the veto was unanimous. All summer long the traffic soared sonorously overhead, the sunlight glinting on struts and tail fins and we waved wildly upwards and boasted that the pilot waved back. In September there was a fatal accident and the pilot was killed. There were no more joy-rides from the aerodrome. The sky was uneventful once more.

Not that excitement was lacking elsewhere. The father of Arthur Jolley, the youngest member of the gang and commonly called Baba, had a greengrocer's shop on the corner of High Lane and Macclesfield Street in which game hung from the ceiling and poultry, due to be slaughtered, lived in the back yard serving time in chicken-wire stockades until set free by Mr Jolley's axe. Our reward for running errands and helping in the stock room was to be allowed to watch the executions. Mr Jolley was a powerful man with hands as red as if they had been steeped in a pail of cold water. He killed hens by wringing their necks. One quick, clockwise twist and the bird went limp, its eyes skinned over, its wings buffetted Mr Jolley's legs for a moment, then slowed down until they stirred as languidly as a lady's fan. Ducks, geese and cockerels he decapitated. They were tougher, he explained, more difficult to deal with. He sounded very scientific as though he had made a study of the subject. We sat on a bench by the far wall and watched him place the execution block in position. Normally it was used for chopping firewood – one of the shop's profitable sidelines – but all its scars oozed blood, as old and as black as tar. The neck of the bird was pulled straight and the axe descended. The head was thrown to one side, the body tossed into a zinc bath. Mr Jolley killed as many birds as he and his wife could pluck in the course of one evening. The average number was ten. He was half-way through his quota one afternoon when there was an unexpected diversion. A cockerel which had just been beheaded and thrown on to the pile of corpses suddenly sprang to its feet and ran a circuit of the yard, sprinting between orange crates and dustbins, its bronze neck-feathers pulsing like a ruff, a jet of blood spurting from its severed neck and trailing briefly in the air like a banner. Mr Jolley stooped to catch it and slipped. The cockerel ran through his out-stretched hands and past him, through an open door and into the shop. We heard screams and the crash of falling merchandise. Glass splintered and the cockerel, still jetting like a fountain, ran back into the yard and into Mr Jolley's arms. He gathered the body to his breast, his face gaudy with blood and there was a hush as though another axe had fallen somewhere, severing time itself. We sat attentively, awaiting the next move. Mr Jolley shook his head and seemed to see the cockerel for the first time since he had scooped it up. Carefully, almost reverently he put the body into the zinc bath and wiped his face with a sack. 'There'll be no more killing today,' he said, 'get off home.' The floor of the shop was blotched with dark puddles and glacier mints and shards of barley sugar were strewn across the King Edwards like fairy lights. Glancing back into the yard I saw Mr Jolley turn round and round as if still watching the cockerel make its circuit. He put his red hands to his face and covered his eyes.

For several days I said nothing to the gang about going away to school. I feared that by simply making the announcement

I would point to the difference between us and, by doing so, exclude myself from their company. It was like Mr and Mrs Pointon, I thought. Once they had realised how different they were from each other it must have been impossible for them to live together. Finally, I told Robbie Cook.

We had gone to the coal-yards at Smallthorne on a dung-collecting expedition. The coal carts were all drawn by horses, huge brown and grey beasts with nicotined moustaches like drill sergeants and frills of feathery hair about their fetlocks. They gave off a smell like liquorice, a mixture of sweat and coal dust, and their harness was studded with brass shields and badges which winked and glittered as they pulled their loads. We saved apple cores and carrot tops to feed them, flattening our palms and holding our breath as the bristly pink lips took up the offering and tossed it back to be crunched between massive yellow teeth. Their breath was hot and sweet and we inhaled it like incense. Their dung, though, was a source of income. Keen gardeners in the avenue paid a penny a bucket or sixpence for a barrow-load. There was no lack of competitors. The approach road to the coal-yards was often lined with boys clutching shovels and sacks. Each cart as it left the yard and creaked slowly towards the main road had its own retinue, a loyal band of followers who kept pace with the horse, their eyes fixed on its tail. If it lifted in an arc there was a brief cheer, then a scramble for the yellow nuggets that thudded softly to the ground. To fill a barrow took two hours or more.

'I'm going away to boarding school,' I told Robbie. 'I'll be living there with a lot of other lads.'

'Whereabouts?'

'Wolverhampton,' I said. 'Where they make Sunbeam motors.'

He nodded several times, still concentrating on the bend of the road where the next cart would come into view. 'Do you want to go?'

'Not much. My mother says I must.'

'I wouldn't want to go,' he said.

'Why not?'

'I like it here.'

'My mother says it's a great opportunity.'

'Happen it is,' said Robbie. 'If you want that sort of thing.' He looked up as a flock of pigeons wheeled overhead, then fluttered down to settle on the road. They too were interested in the dung, sorting through the cobs mashed by the horse's hooves for grain and undigested flakes of oats. 'Will you have your own study?' he asked. Like me, Robbie read *The Magnet*.

'Share one, most likely.'

'There'll be a lot of whacking, I shouldn't wonder.' He tapped my shoulder. 'Touch your toes, lad. Six of the best.'

'I don't see why,' I said.

'That's what they do at those boarding schools. You've only got to read the books. You remember that tale in *The Hotspur*. Red Circle School with Mr Smugg the Housemaster.' Sympathy made his eyes glisten. 'Rather thee than me,' he said.

'My mother wouldn't let them touch me.'

'She'll have nowt to do with it. She won't be there.'

'I won't be doing anything wrong.'

He laughed mirthlessly. 'Little lads get picked on. And there'll be bullies too.'

'That's just in the books.'

'Oh aye?'

'You don't know for sure,' I said. But we both knew. All boarding schools had bullies. All the books said so. We had it on the authority of *The Magnet* and *The Hotspur*, and mounting apprehension formed a lump in my stomach as heavy as lead, as cold as ice.

'You could run away,' said Robbie.

'Now, you mean?'

'From the school.'

'Where would I go?'

'You could come home.'

'That wouldn't work,' I said. 'They'd send me back. You know what they're like.'

A coal cart creaked round the corner and he seized the handles of his barrow. 'Tha'll have to put up with it then.' He nodded towards the shovel. 'Get hold of it. And don't dig up too much grit. They don't like that on their roses.'

Already his mind was on the business in hand and I was left with the monsters he had summoned up. The horse's tail arched and, aromatic and gilded, the dung descended as perfect as a clutch of new-laid eggs. As I shovelled it up the dismal thought struck me that, being away at school, I would never see the roses it was going to feed.

Signs of my imminent departure multiplied. My mother sat at the dining table carefully printing my name on strips of tape with marking ink. They were to be stitched inside vests and underpants, stuck on to the back of my hairbrush and on to the lid of my pencil box. I visited our GP for the inoculations specified by the school infirmary. My head was examined for nits. My toe-nails were cut. My mother stamped and addressed a dozen envelopes for me to write home every Sunday. I was presented with a prayer book and a new Bible. Timetables were consulted, the train chosen. I was asked what I would like for lunch on my last day at home and after choosing cold rabbit – which Mary served cooked with marjoram, shimmering in its own jelly – I burst into tears, an embarrassment which any reference to the school was likely to provoke.

When the actual morning came, however, apprehension gave way to excitement. I was disgracefully cheerful. To boost my flagging spirits my mother had ordered a taxi to take Mary and myself to Stoke station instead of our going by bus and when she heard me whistling as I brushed my shoes she clicked her tongue. 'Seems I shouldn't have bothered with the taxi,' she said, 'you sound happy enough already.'

I stopped whistling in mid-chorus. 'I'm not.'

'You mean you're putting a brave face on it.'

'I don't know what you mean,' I said. 'You're the one who wants me to go.'

'It's needs must,' said my mother. 'It's not what I want. It's simply the best thing all round.' I showed her my shoes and she pointed to a scrap of mud on the heel of one of them. 'Give it another brush.' I did as I was told and she stroked my hair. 'Think of me tonight,' she said. 'This house will be empty. I shall be on my own.'

My high spirits evaporated. I imagined her sitting on the couch by the dining room window, twilight softening the garden outside, a variety programme on the radio going unheeded. Instantly tears welled up again as if, somewhere in my nose, a pump had been switched on. 'There, there,' said my mother contentedly, 'don't cry.' She tugged a handkerchief from her sleeve and pinched my nose. 'Give it a good blow.' She was not being capricious, I realised. Her mood was as unstable as my own and she needed to direct our parting as she had rehearsed it in her mind. It was how she wished to remember it, how she would describe it to others.

She came to the gate to wave goodbye and through the rear window of the taxi I saw her handkerchief fluttering bravely as we turned the corner of the avenue. On the train I ate a bar of milk chocolate and counted the telegraph poles whizzing by. After two hundred I gave up. I opened the window to look out but Mary hauled me back. 'There's a man I know had his head knocked off doing that,' she said. She was wearing her navy blue silk coat and matching hat with a spray of blue glass cherries. Her dress was a lighter blue and across the neckline she had pinned a vee of lace that she called her modesty vest. It was the same outfit she wore to go on holiday and to attend Harvest Festivals. It was for special occasions and this was one of them. In accompanying me to school she was representing my family. At Wolverhampton station we boarded a tram to Penn Common and out of the corner of my eye I studied the boy sitting opposite. He wore the uniform I had seen in the photograph. It was as extraordinary as I had conceived it to be, but he seemed entirely at ease. The tram sighed to a halt. We got off and as it pulled away I saw a row of iron railings, a gravel drive and the school at the end of it. By the gate there was a large board on which there was painted in gold letters The Royal Orphanage School, Wolverhampton. I read the words again and again but they made no sense. Something was wrong, I thought. There had been a terrible mistake. No one before had ever told me that I was an orphan.

Two

A TEACHER with a ginger moustache and leather patches on the elbows of his sports jacket showed us into the Assembly Hall. There were other boys there already, sitting beside their mothers or aunts or cousins on straight-backed chairs, their feet barely touching the glossy floor. The ceiling was spanned by massive black beams. There was an organ loft and the sunlight spilling through coloured glass arches which topped every window formed patterns on the panelled walls. It was like being in church. We spoke in whispers. One of the women who wore a black linen suit and pill-box hat with a short veil tapped a cigarette on the lid of a silver case. She put it to her lips several times, but she did not light it. Finally she put it away. She saw us watching her. 'There are no ash-trays,' she said.

'Fancy that,' said Mary. She was mesmerised, I knew, by the smartness of it all. She had never before spoken to a lady in black who tapped a cigarette on a silver case.

'They asked us to wait,' said the lady. 'They didn't say for how long.'

'It's just till they get their uniforms,' said Mary. 'That's what the gentleman said.'

'The master, you mean.' I sensed that a small reproof had been delivered. There was a difference between gentlemen and masters.

The silence re-formed. I watched motes of dust spiralling down through the coloured rungs of light. There was a strong smell of floor polish and distantly doors banged and pots clattered as if there were comings and goings in a giant's kitchen. I felt myself shrinking. My bladder began to itch. 'I want the lav,' I whispered in Mary's ear.

'Can't you wait?'

'I want to go badly.'

She clutched her handbag and sighed. 'See if you can find

the man who let us in. Ask him.' The glass cherries on her hat chattered in her agitation. I slid off my chair and walked to the door, my footsteps thunderous on the bare boards. Every head turned to watch me go by.

I found the ginger-moustached master standing in the front porch. 'Yes,' he said. 'What is it?'

'Please sir, I want to be excused.'

'Now? This minute?'

'Yes sir.'

He shot his cuff and glared at his watch. 'I'm waiting for the next tram. There are several more boys still to come.' I crossed my legs and he looked at his watch again. 'All right,' he said. 'Down the corridor. Turn left and it's the first door on your left. Be quick about it and remember that it's the staff cloakroom. Normally you are not allowed to make use of it. This is an emergency.' I turned to go, but he called me back. 'Remember to wash your hands,' he said. 'It's a school rule. We insist on hygiene.'

In the cloak-room I attempted to hit the bulls-eye stamped beneath the glaze on the back of the urinal but it was a target for much taller men. Again I felt I was in the abode of giants. I could barely reach into the wash-basin and I could only dry my hands on the roller towel by reaching high above my head. Water ran down my wrists and soaked my shirt. I combed my hair with my fingers and saw my disembodied hand reflected in the mirror on the wall. Behind me the door was jerked violently open. 'Hurry up boy. It's time to say your goodbyes.'

I buttoned my fly and trotted out into the entrance hall where a mass farewell was taking place. Mary stood to one side her fingers twined, her toes turned inwards and I saw, as if for the first time, the bulge on her left foot, like a pebble wedged beneath the glacé kid, where she said a bunion plagued her. 'Well,' she said, 'it's time to be off. There's a train in just under the hour. If I catch that I'll be back in time to get your mother her tea.'

The vision of that distant house, stilled now without my presence, where my mother sat staring blindly into the garden was unbearable. 'Tell her I love her,' I gulped.

She patted my cheek as if she felt it improper to

demonstrate any more emotion. 'She knows that.'

'I shall hate it here.'

'No you won't,' she said. 'You don't know what it's like. It looks grand to me.'

We were both intimidated. But she, I realised, was awed not only by the size and resonance of the building which made small sounds significant and, at the same time, diminished the person who uttered them; she was also embarrassed by the company, afraid that she might say the wrong thing or make the wrong move. Instinctively she knew that, after she had gone, I would be held responsible for any falling short on her part. Not only my family's good name was at stake; so was my standing within the group. By keeping her distance she was committing me to nothing. 'The master seemed very nice,' she said. 'If they're all as obliging as that you've no cause to fret.'

I swallowed hard. 'I suppose not.'

'They say they'll be packing your own clothes for you to bring home at the end of term.'

'I see.'

'I'm sorry I didn't see you in your uniform. Your mother would have liked that.' She began to put on her gloves. They were made of knitted black silk, like the net that my Aunt Ada put over her currant bushes to protect them against birds. On the right glove, I noticed, she had cut off the top flap of the middle finger and sewn it up so that the stump was bisected by a neatly-turned seam. 'You'd better catch your train,' I said. 'Thank you for coming with me.'

'There wasn't anyone else,' said Mary. 'I'm glad I was asked.' She settled her hat firmly on her shimmering hair and kissed me briskly on each cheek. 'Be a good lad,' she said. 'Make us all proud of you.' The master held the door open for her and without looking back she marched out, down the steps and along the drive, staggering slightly on the pebbles as if she was wading through deep snow. I saw her cross the road and position herself by the tram stop. I waved once before the tram cut off my view but she did not wave back.

'It's Oakes, isn't it?' said the master with the ginger moustache and when I nodded he made a tick on a list he had clipped to a board. 'Cut along to the sewing room,' he said. 'Follow the rest of the boys upstairs. Don't dawdle.'

I climbed the broad staircase and saw an open door on the first landing. By a table stacked high with grey flannel trousers stood a line of boys wearing only their shirts and socks. Some of them had their hands clasped modestly in front of them. Others had tucked the front flap of their shirts between their legs. They all seemed subdued; several had tear marks streaking their faces. A large lady in a blue smock, whose startling yellow hair was coiled into a bun on the back of her head sat behind the table dispensing underpants and shorts. 'You'll see that the underpants have loops at the front on either side,' she said. 'That's for your braces to go through. When you button them on to your trousers they keep the underpants up. Does everyone understand?' There were no dissenting voices and she nodded, not unpleasantly I thought, but as if any hesitation on the part of her audience would not be well received. 'Belts are not permitted,' she continued. 'The headmaster believes that they interfere with your digestion and squeeze your insides into knots. Anyone found wearing a belt will have it confiscated.'

Two other ladies in blue smocks beckoned me towards them. They sat in the bay of a large semi-circular window which arched from floor to ceiling. The panes were leaded and through them I saw the front drive and beyond it, trams gliding along the main road. We were under the eaves. There was an open fire in the grate and a kettle steamed on the hob. It seemed improbably cosy; a proper house which existed secretly within the giant's castle. 'What's your name, then?' enquired the lady with a long, hand-written list in her lap.

'Philip Oakes,' I said.

'Just Oakes will do,' she said, running her finger down the column. 'We don't use first names here.' She made a tick in the appropriate place and checked the entry against a corresponding list in a large red ledger. 'Right,' she said, 'they've put you into Lees House and your school number is thirty-nine..That's the number of your bed and your locker. Make sure you remember it.' She nodded to her companion and as she inclined her head firelight flooded her gold-rimmed spectacles. 'Give me a shirt, Marjorie. A small one I should think.' She tapped the waistband of my trousers with her index finger. 'Take those off and leave them here. And your underpants and shoes. They'll go in your case for safe-keeping.' I fumbled with my buttons and without waiting she undid them for me, peeling off my clothes with practised hands so that before I knew it I stood naked between her blue-draped knees. A new grey shirt was slipped over my head. She fastened the collar then patted my behind. 'Off you go then,' she said. 'Don't dilly-dally.' All three women laughed and I joined the queue at the first table. I was handed underpants and trousers and I put them on, balancing on one leg and finding splinters on the un-carpeted floor. At another table I was fitted with shoes; at another I was given a khaki handkerchief and a black and yellow striped tie. The lady with gold-rimmed spectacles gave us blazers and showed us how to pin the school badge, a metal shield bearing the motto *Nisi Dominus Frustra*, to the breast pocket. 'It's Latin,' she said. 'It means "Without the help of the Lord we build in vain". You should remember that too.'

The master with the ginger moustache put his head round the door. 'How are we doing, Mrs Dove?' he asked.

'All done, Mr Granger,' said the lady with yellow hair and in single file we were marched along the landing to a door masked in green baize and studded with brass pins. 'Unless you have business here, this part of the school is out of bounds,' he said. 'So are the dormitories during the day, except for thirty minutes between the end of lunch and the commencement of afternoon classes. If there are any articles you may need during the day you must remember to take them with you when you make your beds after breakfast.' He allowed us a fleeting smile. 'I know it must seem a great deal to remember but there is a reason for everything. We live by the rules. Rules are the railway lines of life.' He unlocked the door and ushered us into the main dormitory. 'Now,' he said 'are there any questions?'

'Please sir,' said a small plump boy with shiny red cheeks. 'Why is the rest of the school out of bounds?'

'Name?'

'Minton, sir.'

'The reason, Minton,' said Mr Granger, 'is that beyond the sewing room where you have just been equipped with your school uniform lies the girls' wing of this establishment. We enjoy a friendly relationship but we do not fraternize. Are you familiar with the word?'

'No sir.'

'It means to associate or to behave as intimates with. Is that clear?'

Minton nodded. 'Thank you, sir.'

'Anyone else?'

'What about uniforms, sir? When do we have to wear the cloaks?'

'Name?'

'Fisher, sir.'

'The cloaks, Fisher, are part of the highly esteemed tradition of the school to which you should feel proud to belong. You will, in fact, wear the uniform to church on Sundays and on your excursions outside the school.' He raised a warning finger. 'I have, on occasion, heard boys criticize the uniform. But it is the badge of your school, just as surely as the badge which you wear on your blazer pocket. Boys here have worn it for nearly one hundred years. It is living history.' Mr Granger blew his nose and spent some time tucking his handkerchief back into his jacket sleeve. 'As I have already intimated, this takes time to learn,' he continued. 'But I feel – and I know that the headmaster also feels – it is a vital part of your education. It is the best we have to offer. It is a lesson which goes beyond the classroom.'

There were eight of us grouped round him in a semi-circle. On either side of us stood rows of beds covered with red blankets on which the school monogram was emblazoned. At the foot of each bed was a locker bearing a number. The ceilings were high and electric lights with shades like coolie's hats hung from the beams. The floor was uncarpeted and our heels squeaked on the pale waxed oak. At one end of the dormitory a varnished cabin had been built into the angle of the two walls. 'That is where your dormitory master sleeps,' said Mr Granger. 'He is there to solve any problem which may arise and also to maintain discipline. He is, so to speak, the captain of this particular ship.'

The analogy was fitting. The cabin door had a single round window like a porthole and beneath it there was a brass name-plate into which a visiting card was slotted. The name on the card was 'Frank Smith'. There were no letters after the name. He told us so himself when he sauntered into the dormitory five minutes later, two tennis rackets – each in a waterproof cover – tucked under his arm and a school porter puffing behind him, a large hide suitcase balanced on one shoulder. 'In there,' said Mr Smith nodding towards the cabin. 'Don't drop it. *Set* it down gently.' He had a flat northern accent which smacked the vowels like a hand on wet flesh. The porter slid the case off his shoulder and massaged his neck. 'What about the rest?' he enquired.

'Bring them up when they arrive.' Mr Smith took a handful of change from his pocket and picked out a sixpenny piece which he spun in the air and grabbed as the porter reached out for it. 'You need to be faster than that,' he said. He spun the coin again and allowed the porter to catch it. 'You'd never do in the slips,' he said, 'they'd drive holes through you.' The porter pocketed the coin and shuffled away. 'Right through you,' Mr Smith called after him. He leaned against the wall of the cabin and looked us over. 'Do any of you play cricket?'

'I do, sir,' said Minton.

'Do you now. Anyone else?'

There was an awkward silence. 'What have we got here, Mr Granger?' he demanded. 'Not sportsmen at any rate.'

'They're just new boys,' said Mr Granger. He seemed as ill at ease as we were.

'I can see they're new boys,' said Mr Smith. 'That much is clear. Even to me. Even without being told. But what else are they, I wonder.' He was taller than Mr Granger and nattily dressed in dark grey flannels and a black barathea blazer with brass buttons. He wore a white shirt and striped red and gold tie. His hair was brilliantined and the parting seemed to have been gouged in the gilt cap which covered his head. His complexion was dark red, baked like a brick and rough as if it had been scoured by sun and wind. He smelled of cigarette smoke and some kind of liniment. He put a fist to his mouth and belched softly into it. 'Manners,' he said.

'I'm just settling the boys in,' said Mr Granger.

Mr Smith braced himself against the cabin wall. 'Better tell them who I am.' Very carefully he edged himself up until he stood erect. The smell of liniment hung in the air and he peeled the silver paper from a tube of peppermints and popped one into his mouth. He sucked it loudly. 'Tell them,' he said.

I stared at his brogues, punched and tasselled like a lace doily. Many hours and tins of polish had gone into producing their high gloss. 'This is Mr Smith, our sports master,' said Mr Granger. 'He played cricket for Lancashire.'

'Professionally,' said Mr Smith.

Mr Granger nodded. 'As a professional. As I was about to say.'

'There are no letters after my name,' said Mr Smith. 'I am not a classroom teacher. My job is to teach you how to use your bodies.' He bent his right arm and leaned forward. 'Feel that,' he ordered. 'Feel that muscle.'

Beneath the sleeve of his blazer I felt a bulge like a small cobble stone. 'It's hard,' I said.

'I am a hard man,' said Mr Smith. 'Bear that in mind.'

We all bobbed our heads; Mr Granger too. 'We must hurry along,' he said. 'There's the san to visit yet.'

'Don't let me stop you,' said Mr Smith. He crunched his peppermint and settled himself more securely against the cabin wall. The back of his head seemed to be glued to the varnished wood. If it came unstuck, I thought, he would fold like a blanket. He waved us on, his rough red face relaxing into a smile. 'Off you go,' he said. 'Off and get yourselves seen to.'

Mr Granger led us through another dormitory, down a narrow flight of stairs and into a long corridor. At the far end a wintry pallor showed through a glass-topped door and instinctively we turned towards it like seedlings leaning towards the light. The corridor had an arched roof. The walls were damp to the touch and our fingers left streaks in the condensation. We emerged into a quadrangle with a glass roof and benches against the walls. There was what looked like a ticket office set in one wall, with a padlocked door and a small window covered by a wire grille. 'For your future reference,' said Mr Granger 'that is the tuck shop, open each week-day from 1.15 to 1.45. Only sweets sold by the school are permitted; which means no chewing gum, no bubblegum, no stick jaw.' He indicated an archway ahead of us: 'Through there to the sanatorium.'

The inspection was brief but thorough. Our hair was once again combed for nits, then we were told to take off our shirts, drop our trousers and revolve slowly with our arms raised while the nurse and the matron scrutinized our bodies for any sign of rash. The matron was short and grey-haired and wore what appeared to be a folded tray-cloth on her head. Nurse Tanser had fat red lips and pencilled eyebrows. She wore black stockings on plump legs and a white apron over a butcher-blue dress. Her sleeves were rolled and the cuffs tucked under arm-bands like the paper bracelets which the butcher at home used to decorate his crown of lamb. She took our temperatures, four at a time, plucking the thermometers from a potted-paste jar half-full of milky disinfectant and criss-crossed over the top with strips of sticking plaster. 'Keep the thermometer under your tongue and don't talk,' she said. 'The last boy who talked bit a thermometer in half and swallowed all the mercury.' She held my wrist between cool white fingers to take my pulse. 'Mercury is poisonous,' she said.

Mr Granger was worried about the time. 'It's the head-master's address in five minutes,' he said. 'Down to the Assembly Hall. At the double.' He led the way, trotting down staircases, bustling along corridors and we followed him, tucking in our shirts and attempting to knot our ties as we followed in his wake. The Hall was full. Mr Granger led us to the front row of chairs and I sat down, aware that eyes were studying the back of my neck, conscious of knees nudging me from behind. It seemed at least a year since I had been in the Hall with Mary. She would still be on the train, I thought, hands folded in her lap, watching the houses and fields and creatures speed by, already planning the evening meal for herself and my mother.

In front of us the staff sat on either side of a brass lectern. All of them, except Mr Smith, wore gowns. His chin was resting on his chest and he studied his finger nails intently. At the piano sat a teacher with dark, frizzy hair and a moustache as fine as Nurse Tanser's eyebrows. He glanced towards the back of the hall and, in response to an unseen signal, struck a resounding chord. Everyone stood up and down the centre aisle strode the headmaster, walking so vigorously that behind him his gown streamed level with the floor. He was followed by his wife, a plump lady wearing a dress patterned with cornflowers and behind her scampered a small brown dog. She scooped it up when they reached the dais and settled it in her lap. The headmaster spread his papers on the lectern and cleared his throat. His head was thrust back as if to counterbalance the perfect pot of his belly which strained at the buttons of his waistcoat. A gold watch-chain traced the lower circumference and a row of pens in his top pocket fenced off the start of the tumulus. His face was a light mauve. He wore rimless glasses and his scalp shone through his thinning hair. His name, as I already knew, was George Gibbs. My mother, who had once been a soprano with the North Staffs Choir, admired him as a singer. He performed regularly on the wireless as The Midlands Baritone, specialising in ballads, sea shanties and selections from Gilbert and Sullivan. He faced us now as I imagined he would face an audience, perfectly still, waiting for the last scuffle, the final whisper to die away. He spread his hands in a gesture of welcome or benediction. 'Good afternoon, boys,' he said. 'Good afternoon, sir,' growled the school in reply.

'To mark the beginning of another term we will sing the hymn "Lord admit us with Thy blessing",' said Mr Gibbs. 'I want everyone singing. No mumblers. Throw out your chests and open your mouths.'

He set the example he wished us to follow, balancing the hymn book on his open palm and using it as a surface on which to skim his volley of song so that his voice reached every corner of the hall.

The amount of pure noise was amazing. Sitting only a few feet away from Mr Gibbs I watched his mauve cheeks quiver like the flanks of a horse as he pumped out words and music. He outsang his staff. He outsang his pupils. When the hymn ended it was Mr Gibbs who laid it to rest, sustaining the last golden note long after the other singers had run out of breath, keeping it aloft effortlessly until it died of its own sweetness. He closed his eyes for a moment as though the sensation was too much to bear, but when he opened them again he was transformed. 'This term,' he said, without preamble, 'there will be no litter. I want no sweet wrappers, no silver paper, no comics left on any exposed surface. If they are abandoned for others to pick up they constitute litter. And anyone creating litter will be punished.' He paused for effect. 'I shall treat forms and dormitories as I would treat individuals. Each member of this school is responsible for its tidiness or otherwise and I shall take swift and drastic action if my instructions are disobeyed.'

He put his hands flat on the lectern and I thought what a substantial figure he made. His high colour, his bulk, the black folds of his gown gave him total authority. 'Smoking,' said Mr Gibbs. 'It is a habit to which I am myself addicted. I am not proud of the fact, although in my case I think there is some excuse. I smoked my first cigarette on the Somme in 1916. I was then a young and inexperienced army officer and the Boche was trying to ensure that I grew no older or wiser.' There was a soft ripple of laughter, spelling no particular amusement but acknowledging a line like a familiar landmark on a journey frequently taken. Smoking and the part he had played in the First World War was a theme upon which Mr Gibbs waxed eloquent. He told us about men under stress and about a padre named Woodbine Willie who travelled the trenches dispensing faith and cigarettes to mud-stained Tommies. 'That,' said Mr Gibbs, almost singing the words, 'was Christianity in its highest form.' He eyed us sternly. 'But smoking in this school is quite another matter. It is harmful to your health. It is wasteful to your pocket. It leads to slackness and conspiracy. And it will cease! Boys who are reported to me for smoking will be caned, whatever their age or excuse. If they are reported a second time they will be expelled.' He tugged the folds of his gown about him, drawing the shutters on his edict, admitting no further argument.

For some time he continued to spell out the business of the school, listing football fixtures, film shows and lectures, and I saw that behind him Mr Smith was asleep, a fine thread of spittle darkening his tie, his breathing sonorous. Mrs Gibbs nudged him sharply and his head jerked upright. 'We have several new boys with us this term,' said Mr Gibbs, 'and I have no doubt that, at the moment – like myself in France – they are feeling lost and far from home. Let me assure them that the feeling will soon pass. They now belong to a tradition which we all share. It will instruct them and sustain them. They, in turn, must work hard, follow the rules and play the game.' As he spoke the words the late afternoon sun blazed once through the stained glass and then dimmed. It was as though a prayer had been uttered and answered. The guardians of the place were present. I could sense them there; white-flannelled, noble-browed, British to the core. Mr Smith snored gently and the headmaster glared at him over his shoulder. 'We will sing the hymn "Fight the good fight with all thy might",' he said. The piano struck the opening chord and we all stood up. Mr Smith lurched to his feet seconds later and as the music pummelled him awake I saw his lips moving stiffly in mime. A lock of hair had come unstuck and jutted from his head like a loose plank. He smoothed it down but it sprang up again. He blinked hard, pressing his eyeballs back into his skull, then stared ahead as the assembly shuddered into focus. The hymn came to an end with Mr Gibbs once again cementing the final note and we stood with our heads bowed as the staff filed out. Mr Smith brought up the rear of the column, his confidence restored, his brogues chiming the length of the aisle.

The hall doors swung shut and someone dug me in the back. I turned round to see a boy slightly older than myself with his index finger now aimed at my stomach.

'Have they put you in Lees?' he demanded.

I fingered my tie. 'Yes, they have.'

'Can you play soccer?'

'Not much.'

'Can you box?'

'I've never tried.'

'Any good at athletics?'

'What do you mean?'

'Running, jumping, hurdles, throwing the javelin.'

'I can run,' I said, playing safe.

'Sprinter or long distance?'

'Sprinter,' I said.

He eyed me sceptically. 'What's your name?' I told him but he did not seem impressed. 'You're not from London, are you.' It was not a question, but a statement of fact. As I was to learn over the next few days a certain prestige was attached to where you lived. To be metropolitan was best; failing that, a country address in a region which had romantic or historical associations such as Devon, came a good second. To be provincial as I was earned the lowest rating of all.

Mr Granger bustled forward, his sheaf of papers clasped to his breast. He stood in front of the lectern not presuming to usurp the headmaster's rightful place and clapped his hands for silence. 'We will now proceed to the dining hall,' he said. 'There will not be a stampede. You will leave assembly row by row and you will walk, not run along the corridors.' He clapped his hands again. 'I will repeat that. You will walk and not run. Prefects will take the name of any boy they see running.' He nodded briskly. 'The first row will lead off. From the front.'

I was jogged into line, the boy behind me treading on my heels and propelled into the corridor where the walk quickened into a trot and the trot became a gallop. I found myself running with the rest, racing through a stone labyrinth while prefects behind us bellowed threats and somewhere ahead of us other voices roared admonitions. The boy who had prodded me in the back ran past me.

'Call yourself a sprinter,' he panted.

I pelted after him. 'As good as you.'

A boy ahead of us tripped and fell and suddenly there was a log-jam of bodies into which I tumbled. A hand grabbed the collar of my blazer and hauled me to my feet. 'Come on,' said the pace-maker, 'before they put us on report.'

'What's that?'

'Never mind. Just get a move on.'

We turned the corner and behind us the prefects swooped on the casualties who had been slow to recover. 'By the way,' said my new friend, 'my name's Carpenter.' We solemnly shook hands and walked swiftly but sedately into the dining hall.

Three

WEEKS later, when I went home for the Easter holiday, my mother asked me what school food was like. 'Disgusting,' I said. But it was only a fraction of the truth, as inadequate as describing Don Bradman as an Australian or Dr Buck Ruxton as a physician. The school menu was a kind of melodrama and could only be described in the terms we applied to the greatest cricketer alive or the most notorious murderer who not only killed his wife but dismembered her, then parcelled up her limbs like choice cuts. We had an appetite for horror and each day it was gratified by what emerged from the school kitchens.

There was, for instance, a variety of brawn in which were entombed scrolls of fat and remnants of flesh which looked as though they had been salvaged from a fearful explosion. Some of the remnants bore bristles and the autopsies which were performed each time the brawn appeared, pink and quaking on our plates, produced a wide range of theories as to what the animal had been when it was alive. There were no bones on which to base our investigations, only shavings of gristle and multi-coloured sections of sinews and blood vessels, stained like the specimens we peered at through the miscroscope in biology lessons. Some of us opted for horse. One morbid class-mate who claimed that he had once found a finger-nail in his helping, argued strongly that the remains were human. But the consensus of opinion held that the brawn was principally pig and Pig was what it was called from that day on.

Liver was known as Beast. It was served on large trays, one to each table, in which thick slices of offal perforated by veins the diameter of a lead pencil lay half-submerged in gravy. The slices were stacked sideways like tiles waiting to be pegged to a roof and between them blood had clotted and cooked into a sleek fawn jelly. It was not a popular meal.

Nor was stew which was designated Scum. Its ingredients defied analysis. Pig could, at least, be separated into hide and hair but the component parts of Scum had metamorphosed during cooking into a substance unrelated to anything recognisably animal or vegetable. Poured over mashed potato it reminded me of those photographs of Pompeii in which a man or a woman had been overtaken by the flood of molten lava and died, their hands reaching out through the crust of pumice which encased them. It was an image which regularly spoiled my lunchtime.

Bread was Wodge, margarine was Scrape and tea was Brew. It was drawn from vast urns into metal pots and poured out by the head boy at each table. It tasted invariably of chipped enamel and left a sediment like brick dust at the bottom of the cup. Twice a week we had Squashed Fly Cake, a moist yellow confection clotted with currants, and on winter Saturdays we had Greasy Gobby, a pudding in which sultanas and half-melted blobs of suet clung together, congealing on thick white plates. Occasionally we had Frogspawn, a sago pudding made of translucent balls as big as marbles and, to keep us regular, prunes which had split their skins and lay disembowelled in their own juice.

It was food designed as fuel and we ate it voraciously, stoking our stomachs like boilers, complaining but always greedy for more. It was not like eating at home. Not only the food was different; so was the thought which went into its selection and preparation. My mother was not a simple woman but her attitude towards everything we ate and drank verged on the superstitious. She believed devoutly that it was either Good or Bad; Good, that is, in a moral sense. In her book of rules bread was Good. Beneath the golden crust the wheat was sanctified. Sometimes she would crumble it in her hands and breathe in the essence as if she was taking part in the sacrament. Porridge was good. So was home-made soup with its ballast of pearl barley, its surface molten with beads of fat. I asked her once what it was that winked in my spoon and without hesitation she told me: 'Goodness'. She disapproved of caviar which she had never tasted and of game which, to her, was simply meat festering rotten. 'They hang it until it's *crawling*,' she said, and in my imagination furred and feathered carcases dangled from hooks, dispensing maggots like marrow pips.

At home we ate at the dining room table, a red mahogany slab which had belonged to my mother's parents and which she kept although it was far too large for the house because, she said, it was the only piece of furniture big enough for the entire family to sit around. At school the tables were long and narrow and covered with a green composition like putty which generations of diners had furrowed with their forks, inscribing their initials and tracing grids for noughts and crosses, a game we played using peas as counters, mashing them flat at the end of the meal. There were fifteen tables and twenty boys sat at each of them. There was a serving counter behind which four women wearing white caps and overalls stood as if manning a barricade. And at the far end of the room there was a glass-fronted cabinet containing salt cellars and egg boxes. As I sat down next to Carpenter on that first day a succession of boys went to the cabinet where a master handed them each an egg which they then took to the serving counter. One of the women spooned it into a huge saucepan of boiling water and when it was done, put it into an egg-cup which the boy bore back to his table. One of the lucky ones sat opposite me.

'Matthews and Baldwin get my tops this term,' he said.

'Sucking up to Matthews, are you?' said Carpenter.

'Course not.'

'Not much.'

'Matthews is my friend,' said the boy with the egg. He sliced off the top and passed it across the table to a sandy-haired boy, much bigger than the rest of us.

'Matthews can box,' Carpenter whispered in my ear. 'He broke someone's nose last term.'

'Why haven't we got eggs?' I asked.

'Did your mother pay for them?'

I shook my head. 'I didn't know she had to.'

'Five shillings a term extra. You get two eggs a week.'

I watched Matthews spread four slices of bread with margarine. He spooned the white out of the egg top and carefully divided it into four sections, then placed one section in the exact centre of each piece of bread. Holding his knife like a scalpel he diced the egg white and distributed it over the margarine. He sprinkled it with salt, then pepper, then cut each slice into squares. He dusted his hands as if he had performed some testing operation and delicately with finger and thumb picked up one of the squares and popped it into his mouth. At other tables the same ritual was taking place. There was competition, I realised, to see how long the egg top could be made to last. Tactics varied. At the next table a cup of tea was drunk between each square of bread while Matthews' strategy was to chew each mouthful thirty-two times before swallowing it. I watched the knobs of his jaw muscles rotating beneath his skin like the polished heads of pistons and found myself counting. 'Why don't you have eggs?' I asked Carpenter.

'I don't like them.'

'Me neither,' I lied.

'Think of where they come from,' he said.

'From a hen.'

'From a hen's bum,' he said holding his nose.

We both hooted with laughter and Matthews put down his piece of bread and glanced our way. 'Carpenter's found another moron,' he observed.

'An anti-moron,' said Carpenter.

'Laughing at nothing', said Matthews.

'Laughing at something.'

'Laughing at what?'

'Hens' bums,' said Carpenter and we dissolved into laughter once more.

Matthews screwed his index finger against his temple as if he was drilling a hole. 'Loony,' he said.

Carpenter put a finger to each side of his head and imitated the motion. 'Double loony,' he replied.

I knew instinctively that he had gone too far. Upwards and onwards from Infants' School there were rules for retaliation, unwritten but understood. Cheek was tolerated but the licence was restricted. Strong men were not mocked, heroes were bound to protect their reputations. As Carpenter had already told me, Matthews was a boxer. He clenched his fists and set them on the table as if they were tools to which, by accident, he found himself attached. 'I'll see you outside,' he said. 'In the quad. Don't make me come looking for you.'

'What's wrong with you?' demanded Carpenter. He looked appealingly up and down the table. 'What's wrong with him?' His appetite suddenly vanished. A slice of bread and jam with one bite taken out of it lay abandoned on his plate. 'Can't take a joke,' he complained. 'No sense of humour.'

Matthews returned to his bread-with-egg. He stared stolidly ahead, his jaws churning, his fists resting dangerously on either side of his plate. I tugged Carpenter's sleeve. 'Why not say you're sorry?'

'Can't do that.'

'Why not?'

'They'll say I'm a funk.'

I measured Matthews' broad shoulders against Carpenter's much slighter frame. 'It's better than getting bashed.'

Carpenter shook his head. 'You don't understand. You're a new kid.'

The tables were beginning to empty and in twos and threes boys drifted into the corridor. No one at our table made a move. Over a rubble of gnawed crusts and half-empty cups they watched Matthews complete his meal. The last square of bread was placed carefully into his mouth. His jaws meshed thirty-two times. He drained his cup and replaced it in his saucer. Then, without looking at Carpenter, he rose, stepped over the bench and walked towards the door. 'He's not bothering,' I said.

'He's gone to the quad,' said Carpenter. 'He'll be waiting for me there.'

'You don't have to go.'

'Of course I do. If I don't show up he'll send the pack after me. I'll get scragged.'

'What's the pack?'

'They search you out. They know the places to hide.'

The boy who had given the egg top to Matthews slid his legs over the bench. 'Shall I tell him you're coming?'

'Stop sucking up,' said Carpenter. He stripped off his tie, rolled it up like a caterpillar and put it into his blazer pocket. 'I don't want blood on it,' he said.

I walked with him to the quadrangle. It was like entering an aquarium. A cold light seeped through the glass roof and the flagstones were greasy as if dew had been sucked up through the granite. Matthews stood with his back to the wall. His hands were in his pockets and his face was burnished with the kind of holy vacancy that I remembered settling like a mask on the minister from our chapel at home when he prayed for our souls. It was the look of dedication. Twenty or more boys stirred themselves from the corners in which they had been lounging and formed a circle around us. Ceremoniously Matthews took off his blazer and, rejecting eager hands which offered to hold it, laid it on the bench, straightening the lapels and smoothing a crease from one of the sleeves.

'Do you want me to hold yours?' I asked Carpenter.

'No thank you,' he said politely. He seemed quite unconcerned, even when someone shoved him in the back and he lurched forward, almost colliding with Matthews who had adopted a boxing stance, his guard up, his left fist inclined. Carpenter's hands remained by his sides. He sniffed loudly but did not reach for his handkerchief. Matthews punched him in the chest, not hard but briskly, as if to remind him what was expected of them both. Carpenter shook his head. 'I'm not fighting you,' he said.

'You have to,' said Matthews.

'No I don't', said Carpenter. 'I know you can beat me. What's the point?'

The crowd had grown considerably. 'Funky,' someone shouted, but Carpenter ignored him.

Matthews advanced on his toes, dancing from side to side. He slapped Carpenter's face with his open hand, then danced back, bobbing and weaving as if he was in an exhibition match. A red print of his palm bloomed on Carpenter's cheek like a transfer on a cup and Carpenter traced the outline with his fingertips. He shuffled back a few steps and Matthews came after him, jabbing with his left fist, demonstrating that he could hit Carpenter wherever and whenever he liked. It was obvious, even to me, that he did not wish to inflict pain, merely prove his superiority. To get the demonstration over with he needed Carpenter's help, a token show of retaliation which would absolve him of the charge of being a bully. He smacked the other side of Carpenter's face then actually smiled as Carpenter, with a cry – as much of exasperation as despair – grabbed him round the waist and threw them both against the wall. The back of Matthews' head struck the bricks with an almost musical note like the sound produced by rapping a baulk of timber with a mallet and he slid to the ground taking Carpenter with him. Carpenter was first on his feet. He stooped over the bigger boy, then stepped back. 'He's bleeding,' he announced. 'His head's cut.'

'He'd have beaten you,' said one of the spectators.

'If we'd gone on he'd have beaten me,' said Carpenter. 'This was an accident.' He tugged my sleeve. 'Help me take him to the infirmary.'

We hauled Matthews upright and draped his arms about our necks. 'I can manage,' he said crossly.

'Your head's cut. Matron ought to see it.'

'No need for you to come.'

'But I did it,' said Carpenter. 'I should explain how it happened.'

Matthews blinked hard and removed his arms from our shoulders. 'I've already told you', he said, 'there's no need.' He dabbed the back of his head with a handkerchief and inspected the size of the resulting bloodstain. Several other boys pressed forward to see. 'It's not serious,' said Matthews. 'All it needs is cold water.' He turned to go and then turned back. 'We're evens,' he told Carpenter. 'Don't be so cheeky next time.'

'Sorry Matthews.'

'Shake hands.'

They shook hands and the crowd dispersed, the greater part of it following Matthews as he made for the ablutions to bathe his head. 'Who really won?' I asked.

'I didn't lose,' replied Carpenter, a trifle enigmatically I thought.

'But you didn't fight him.'

'Not strictly speaking.'

'You *told* him you wouldn't fight him,' I insisted.

Carpenter's smile assumed the lineaments of superiority

which I came to recognise as the look of a veteran who had survived a year or more in the trenches. 'Matthews doesn't believe that. Not now. He didn't want me to tell matron what happened either. He knows he'd look pretty silly.'

'Did you work all that out?'

'More or less.'

'Not right away.'

'Not right away,' he agreed. 'You have to watch for openings. You'll learn.'

We walked from the quadrangle into the main playground, an asphalt plain bounded on one side by the school buildings and directly opposite by a high wall. At the top of the yard there was a lower wall embroidered with barbed wire and behind it a row of houses. Lights shone through curtained windows; a plume of smoke rose calmly from one chimney; a car engine crooned and a dog barked. Only a few hundred yards away another world was going about its business. It had nothing to do with me. On the other side of the wall no one knew that I existed.

'Did you bring any tuck?' asked Carpenter.

'There was some chocolate in my suit-case.'

He sighed in commiseration. 'They'll have pinched it. Those hags in the sewing room pinch everything.'

'They can't do that.'

'We're not supposed to bring tuck in with us. They'll just say they've confiscated it.' He stared at the darkening sky which seemed to hang over the playground like a bell jar. 'What sweets do you like best?' he enquired.

I thought of Wonderbars and both kinds of Palm toffee, chocolate and banana split. I thought of aniseed balls and farthing chews and gob-stoppers which changed colour five times before dissolving. I thought of nougat streaked like Connemara marble, and liquorice as bright as anthracite, which we splintered and steeped in water to make a summer drink. I thought of bubblegum which could be blown into huge pink wens which burst with a satisfying crack, and tiger nuts, as horny and withered as nail parings – and it was impossible to choose between them. Their remembered flavours all seemed to me ambrosial. 'I don't know,' I said, 'what about you?'

Carpenter did not hesitate for a moment. 'Fry's Chocolate Cream.'

'What about Walnut Whips?'

'They're all right,' he conceded, 'so long as you save the walnut till last. You need practice.'

We had reached the centre of the playground. At intervals I saw that the walls were painted with cricket stumps and the ground itself was squared off into football pitches. 'Smithy had that done last term,' said Carpenter. 'You don't want to let him catch you sitting down. He'll have you in a team right off. He can't bear to see you doing nothing.'

'I met him this afternoon,' I said. 'He told us he had no letters after his name.'

Carpenter hooted with laughter and tapped his forehead. 'He's solid bone. Thick all the way through. He's no need to worry though. He's Mrs Gibbs' cousin. She got him the job.'

'Did he really play for Lancashire?'

'Oh yes, that's true enough. He won't let you forget it either. He doesn't like being got out. He likes making runs.' He made a stroke with an imaginary bat. 'Out to the boundary, hero of the side, three centuries last season. Against the juniors, that is.'

'He's my dormitory master.'

'Mine too,' said Carpenter. 'What's your number?'

'Thirty-nine.'

'Right across the dorm from me.' The school clock struck five and a flock of starlings sprayed up from the ivy where they had been roosting. Carpenter unrolled his tie and cracked it like a whip, aiming it at the birds as they wheeled overhead. 'Did you ever see Lash La Rue?' he asked. 'I saw one of his pictures at Christmas. They all had guns and he had just this whip.' He cracked his tie again and a score of enemies bit the dust. 'What's your best picture?' he asked.

I saw myself in the Palace balcony, a Victory lozenge fuming in my mouth, while on the screen mighty Paul Robeson urged his war canoe through the Zambezi rapids. 'Sanders of the River,' I said.

Carpenter nodded judiciously. 'Not bad.' He furled his tie and put it back in his pocket. 'What about cowboys. Tom Mix or Ken Maynard?'

'Tom Mix.'

'And Tony,' said Carpenter, reining an imaginary horse and rearing backwards. His feet marked time on the asphalt and then he was away, steed and rider in one, galloping towards the top of the playground, his breath smoking in the last light. The dusk swallowed him. I could hear him in the distance, snorting and neighing and I slapped my thigh and cantered off to join him. We leaned against the wall puffing comfortably. Across the playground the school shone like an enormous lantern. I could not count the windows. They were yellow holes punched in the brickwork; rows of them, large and small. Heads moved across them. A boy sat at a desk writing a letter, another held a football shirt to his chest. In the gathering darkness we were spies, keeping watch on an unsuspecting army. I made a pistol of my fingers and took aim at a figure gazing out of the dormitory. 'Got him,' I said.

'You'd have missed from here,' said Carpenter. 'Hand guns are no good over twenty feet. Gibbo told us that.'

'How does he know?'

'He was in the war fighting Jerries. You heard him. He's got a medal.'

'I've got two step-brothers who were in the war,' I said. 'They were in the infantry.'

'Did they get wounded?'

I had no idea. 'I expect so,' I said.

Carpenter sighed deeply. 'There's a roll of honour in the chapel. Fifteen old boys killed and twenty wounded. They say prayers for them on Remembrance Day. Gibbo wears his uniform. Riding boots and a Sam Brown.'

'What's that?'

'A belt,' said Carpenter sketching a line diagonally across his chest. 'Frightfully pukka.' He clicked his tongue and suddenly he was a horse again. He pawed the ground and snorted through his nostrils. 'Race you to the bottom.'

We thundered across the playground and through the quadrangle. Carpenter plunged down a dimly lit corridor and I followed him. He burst through a door and, still in pursuit, I found myself in a room in which wash-basins stood in glossy ranks. Brass taps shone like fillings in an endless row of teeth and there was a smell of hot flannels, chlorine and carbolic soap. In one corner there was a large square bath lined with red tiles. Around the walls towels hung on numbered hooks. The light was brilliant, bouncing from porcelain to mirrors and back again. A group of boys, stripped to the waist, their braces dangling like stirrups, stood in line dreamily soaping their necks. Two more brushed their teeth, pausing occasionally to inspect their progress in a mirror. A boy on his own combed his hair, trying first a centre parting, then raking the hair to one side, then the other. Water sung in the pipes. I felt as though I had been admitted to a private club where cleanliness was recreation and vanity was taken seriously. 'These are the ablutions,' said Carpenter.

He led me through the basins to an alcove where, level with our heads, a thick wire cage housed a number of standing tanks. Carpenter slid aside a section of the wire platform and hoisted himself up. He reached down for me and I scrambled after him. He replaced the platform and squeezed between the tanks. 'Watch out,' he said, 'they're hot.' The metal scorched my face and when I swallowed it was like gulping down balls of cotton wool. Carpenter squirmed into the farthest corner and sat with his back to the wall, his head jammed against the ceiling. 'I found this place last term,' he said. 'I come here when I feel like skipping games. It's a good hidey-hole too. The only trouble is you can't keep sweets here. They melt.' He leaned forward and gripped my jaw. 'Don't tell anyone about it. It's a secret.'

'I promise.'

'You need somewhere to go,' said Carpenter, half to himself. 'You'll find that out.'

'I won't tell anyone,' I said. 'I know about secrets.'

He nodded, apparently satisfied. 'You can come by yourself if you like. So long as nobody sees you.'

'I'll take care.'

We remained in the cage until an hour or more later a bell rang. It was shrill, imperative and sustained and even after the sound had died away in the ablutions I could hear its summons in other remote parts of the school. 'It's nothing to worry about,' said Carpenter. 'It's just telling you it's bed-time for juniors.' We burrowed back through the tanks and lowered ourselves through the wire hatch. I watched him slot it back into position, then nonchalantly we strolled into the first alley of basins. Carpenter paused and ran a tap. 'Rinse your face. It's all over dust,' he said. 'Your towel's on your hook. You can get mine while you're at it. Number fifty-two.'

I brought both our towels and washed my face. We used the same red soap to scrub floors at home. I pulled out the plug and was about to swill round the basin but Carpenter stopped me. 'Leave that to the skivvies,' he said, 'they do all the cleaning.'

Mr Granger was waiting in the dormitory still clutching his sheaf of papers. He clapped his hands for silence and we stood by our beds while beyond the uncurtained windows trams roamed up and down the road to the station. 'New boys will be addressed by the headmaster after morning assembly,' he announced. 'As he told you this afternoon we value tidiness in this school. When you undress you will fold your clothes neatly on the locker at the foot of your bed. You will say your prayers kneeling at your bedside. There will be no talking after lights out and no wandering into other dormitories. Do I make myself clear?' There was a grudging murmur of assent and he shot back his cuff to see his watch, a gesture which had become more emphatic as the day progressed. 'You have ten minutes,' he said. 'I shall be back then to turn off the light.' He made a brisk exit and immediately there was a burst of conversation as though the door to an aviary had been unlocked and the room was alive with gossiping birds.

A nightshirt lay across my pillow. It had red and green stripes and a tape bearing the number thirty-nine was sewn to the collar band. When I put it on the hem brushed the floor. Others, I saw, were less fortunate. Some nightshirts reached mid-calf, others ended just below the knees. The boy in the bed to my left was named Burton. He was tall and wiry and when he tugged his shirt over his head it was evident that something had gone wrong in the wash. Irritably and then with mounting desperation he tried to pull down the front and back flaps to cover his buttocks and his genitals. It was an impossible task. The nightshirt had shrunk. If one side was concealed, the other was exposed. He jumped on to his bed and performed a pirouette, extending the front flap of the shirt like a skirt and simpering as he turned. There was a salvo of whistles and catcalls and he blew a kiss into the air and saluted the room with his behind, baring it like a peeled apple.

'Ooh, la la!' shouted someone.

He began to dance, lifting his knees higher and higher until they almost touched his chin. Others imitated him, bouncing on their beds, their legs pumping like a chorus line. Bed springs shrieked, a fine gauze of dust rose in the air. I joined in the dance. I heard myself chanting. A boy opposite missed his footing and crashed to the floor, his shin blazing with blood where he had scored it on the bed frame. I felt as though I had been caught up in a ritual in which the only compulsion was to maintain the rhythm, to make it last, whatever the danger, whatever the fatigue. Sweat prickled on my forehead. I joined hands with Burton and the boy on the bed to my right and we executed high kicks, losing our balance and capsizing on to our backs. I jumped up again and bounced like a ball until, without warning, the door was flung open and Mr Granger strode into the dormitory.

It was as though a switch had been thrown, cutting off the current. The dance died in mid-career. We dived between the sheets and tried vainly to smoothe our blankets. Dust still quivered in the cones of light that leaked from the lamp shades. There was complete silence for a count of ten. I felt my heart thudding in my throat. I bit my pillow until my jaws ached. My feet were deathly cold with damp patches on each instep.

'That exhibition was disgraceful,' said Mr Granger at last. 'I shall not ask for an explanation. Even if I received one it would be beyond belief. All that I have to decide is the nature and the severity of the punishment.' He clasped his hands behind his back and walked the length of the dormitory. At the window he paused to study the distant traffic, then retraced his steps until he stood at the foot of my bed. He prodded my mattress. 'What would you do?'

'I don't know, sir.'

'Nor do I.' He rocked on his heels and I saw his moustache change colour as the light shone through it at different angles. Without it, I thought, he would look a good deal younger. He licked his lips and lowered his head. 'I shall not make a decision tonight,' he said, 'but this entire dormitory is on probation.' He turned slowly, memorizing every face. 'You will be walking a tight-rope,' he declared, stabbing the air with one finger, 'and I shall be watching your every move. Is that understood?' He glared about him fiercely when there was no reply. 'I asked if that was understood,' he said more emphatically. There was a mumble of agreement and Mr Granger nodded as if he shared our relief. 'Very well,' he said. 'On that understanding. There will be no repetition of this appalling behaviour. It depends on you.' He nodded again, nailing the terms of the treaty to an imaginary wall where it hung for us all to study. We had been placed on our honour. He had been excused from reporting – and permitting – a massive breach of discipline. We were in each others debt. We were committed to mutual aid.

Mr Granger tapped the face of his watch. 'Time for lights out. No talking now. Straight to sleep. Goodnight boys.'

'Goodnight sir,' we replied. I closed my eyes and said Our Father. I had not previously intended to say my prayers, but it was a promise I had made to my mother and promises, however long they were to be kept, were in the air that night.

Four

My MOTHER, who was inordinately proud of my treble voice, taught me not to say, but sing the Lord's Prayer. It did not strike me as unusual. My mother's family were all singers and my father was a lay preacher whose appetite for religion and music was gratified each Sunday evening when friends and relations gathered around the piano in the front room to sing favourite hymns. Occasionally the programme was interspersed with arias from The Messiah and Judas Maccabeus and with songs from the Indian Love Lyrics, especially Pale Hands I Loved which was my mother's party piece. They were social gatherings at which my mother served potted-meat sandwiches and biscuits and cups of Camp coffee which came in a bottle bearing a picture of a British officer in India sitting in front of his tent with a sepoy in attendance. My father was a traveller for a pottery firm and at regular intervals he would bring home new lines in crockery on which he would ask our guests to pass an opinion. There was a green and gold tea service which was especially popular. A set of small lustre vases in what was called a 'jazz' pattern, possibly because the design was a violent abstract, was rejected unanimously. In each case my father would report back to his employers. He knew the value of a straw poll. When he was on the road he did not want to waste time peddling goods which had already failed to find favour with the average customer.

His own taste, though, was not always predictable. Sometimes on Sunday evenings when we were singing There Is a Green Hill Far Away or When I Survey the Wondrous Cross, hymns whose sweet melancholy made me ache inside, my eyes would roam around the picture rail where there hung a display of tiles depicting hunting scenes so vivid and bloody that I could never understand how they qualified as decoration. There were hounds tearing out the throat of a stag; a hawk pecking the eyes of a heron; a hare bounding across an undulating heath while all around it small white clouds blossomed from the muzzles of shot-guns aimed by top-hatted hunters. In front of the fire there was a fur rug made from the skin of a polar bear. Swallows swooped across the leaded lights at the top of the bay windows. We kept no pets but the house contained an exotic variety of wild life safely relegated to furniture and fittings.

My father's name was Samuel. He was in his mid-sixties; a short, brusque man with a beaky nose, a neatly clipped moustache and a bald head banked on either side by trim wings of white hair. I did not know him well. He seemed to me immensely old; a contemporary of the God he served. He spent most week-days travelling. He was punctual for appointments, but even more meticulous in his personal habits. Every morning at seven o'clock he would lock him-self in the lavatory with the *News Chronicle*. He would not emerge, my mother told me, until he had successfully moved his bowels, even if it meant missing a train. He was fond of carpentry. A rose trellis that he made and erected remained standing long after his death and I remember sitting with him one afternoon on the back step while he made model crocodiles from plasticine and carved match-sticks into tiny fangs to arm their jaws.

He was a strict man. One day when I grizzled incessantly over some minor disappointment he slapped my face, 'to give me something to cry about'. He was also devout. On Sunday afternoons in summer he took me for walks in the fields at the bottom of the avenue and showed me how to pluck ears of corn from the fields which hemmed the narrow path and strip the husk from the soft white meal inside. The Pharisees had rebuked Jesus for doing precisely that, he said. It was a story which was meant to illustrate the sense and nonsense entailed in keeping the Sabbath holy. Our own rules forbade buying a Sunday paper. But although I tried hard I could not make the connection between Sunday in the Potteries and the distant Palestine Sabbath. When I said so my father would sigh gently, remove the Homburg he habitually wore and after wiping its sweat-band would tell me the story again.

The chapel at which we worshipped was called Hill Top. It was in Burslem and stood on the brow of the first fold of rock which led, like a flight of stairs, from the fuming valley of the Five Towns where pot banks flanked the canal. We were Methodists and our chapel had the severity and the arrogance of a sect which, with some ostentation, rejected the gaudy trappings of other more worldly believers. It was built of granite, dyed black by the soot which filled the air like small dry rain. Its façade was Grecian, its portico supported by a row of stone pillars. Our pew, for which we paid an annual rent, had a square of Axminster carpet on the floor. The choir sat below the organ loft and when they sang anthems I would gaze raptly up at the goitre which throbbed in the throat of Nellie Watkin, our leading soprano.

Nellie was not one of our Sunday evening visitors. She was too grand, too much of a star for such intimate occasions. Our piano stool contained not only hymn books and sheet music but also the *News Chronicle Song Book*, a stout brown volume from which I learned the words of Camp Town Races and Drink to Me Only which I was urged to sing before the hymns began. Most of the men smoked pipes. The women were scented with lavender water and cologne. The pipe smoke and the perfume blended into an agreeable domestic incense which permeated the curtains and the plush of the three-piece suite and even on weekdays I could bury my nose in the uncut moquette and inhale the familiar and reassuring odour of sanctity.

After my father fell ill the piano was rarely played. One of my mother's friends from her early teaching days, a courtesy aunt I knew as Aunt Clara, offered to give me lessons but the exercises were boring and soon came to an end. Scales did not interest me. What I longed to hear were the chords and harmonies which spelled security. It was music I knew by heart. It seemed to me sad and unnatural that my fingers could not produce it simply by striking the keys.

'You have to practise,' said my mother.

I shook my head, my hands tucked beneath my arms.

'If you don't practise you'll never learn.'

'I can't.'

'You mean you won't.

I clamped my arms down more tightly and glared mutinously at the music propped in front of me. I was disappointing everyone, including myself. 'My hands are too small,' I said.

'Rubbish!'

'Perhaps it's too soon,' said Aunt Clara. 'There's plenty of time.'

'The trouble you've taken!' said my mother. 'He's just being rude and ungracious.' She turned her wedding ring around her finger, always a bad sign, and jerked the door open. 'He can just sit there,' she said. 'I don't know what his father would think of him.' It was the ultimate sanction. They went out, leaving me alone. I remained perched on the stool, my legs dangling. I could still hear the music, but it was fainter now.

The piano was played for the last time on the day of my father's funeral. I did not attend the service but waited at home with one of my cousins. I knew I was supposed to be sad, but it was exciting too. When the cars rolled down the avenue, lurching over the bumps and cavities in the unmade road, it was like watching the guests arrive for a party. There was the same smell, the mixture of scent and tobacco smoke. There were the same faces, still smiling but gravely as if they had witnessed something dreadful which they could not share with me. I passed round sandwiches on the green and gold plates. In the dining room my Aunt Ada served sliced ham bought specially from the grocers, Boyce Adams. My Uncle Percy sampled a mouthful and smacked his lips. 'Sweet as a nut,' he said.

When the coffee had been poured everyone assembled in the front room. 'Shall we have a hymn,' proposed my Uncle Arthur, 'one of Sam's favourites.'

My Aunt Ada shook her head vigorously. 'Not a hymn. We've had enough of them for one day.'

'One of his favourite songs then,' said Uncle Arthur.

They all looked at my mother. She blew her nose and tucked the handkerchief in her sleeve. 'If you like,' she said.

The mourners arranged themselves on the three-piece suite and I was gently pushed forward until I was standing beside the piano, pressed against my mother. I could not see her face but I felt her body vibrating like the piano itself when a chord was struck. She sang Sweet and Low and Home Sweet Home and when her voice broke I felt her hands gripping my shoulders as if she feared she would fall. When the song ended the room was perfectly still. Then my mother put down the lid of the piano and locked it. My Uncle Ernest, who I loved best among my relations, drew me aside. 'It's up to you,' he said. 'Tha'll have to take care of her now.' He felt in his pocket and pressed a coin into my hand. By its size and milled edge I knew it was half a crown. I started to thank him but he put his finger to his lips. 'Say nowt. See what you can buy at the fishmonger's.' It was his customary joke, but I had never seen him make it before with such a straight face.

Uncle Ernest was a builder's foreman. As a young man he had emigrated to America, failed to put down roots and returned after a few homesick years. He never talked of his experiences, but in a family so committed to self-improvement he was clearly made to feel that he had let the side down. The impression was reinforced when he joined the building trade and was seen on wind-bitten sites with dirty hands, wearing old clothes. The distinction was plain. He was not a professional person but a working man. If he was hurt by the unspoken disapproval of his brothers and sisters he did not show it, but nurtured an irony that not only protected him but was withering in its contempt for the general point of view. He was a wholly unflustered man. His speech, like all his movements, was deliberate and measured. When he told a story he spun it out, pausing to re-light his pipe before delivering the punch line, then hee-hawing his amusement through wreaths of blue smoke. He never swore, but kept and thickened his Potteries accent so that, at times, it seemed as though he was speaking in another language. His wedding present to my mother and father was a bathroom cabinet which he made out of pear wood. His love of fine carpentry made him a friend of my father and I remember being taken to see his garden gate in which all the sections had been fitted together with twenty different joints. 'There's not a nail there,' he kept repeating. 'It's wood into wood, every inch of it.'

He suffered acutely from bronchitis and rheumatism. His face was the colour of tallow and deeply lined. But I had never seen a man so beautifully dressed. He wore his working clothes like a uniform which he put away when work was done. What I thought of as his real clothes were unlike those worn by any of my other male relatives. His suits were tailor-made; dark worsted and brown flannel pinstripes. His ties were silk and his poplin shirts had soft collars which sat easily on his neck. He wore brown shoes, so dark they were almost black, with a gloss even on the insteps that seemed to repel dirt. His wife, my Aunt Annie, had a soft, cooing voice which reminded me of doves heard on hot summer days. Her skull had been fractured when she was knocked down by a car and her head shaved. When her hair grew again it was entirely white, as fine as spun sugar. She brushed it a hundred times every morning and night and to improve its sheen rubbed it with a silk scarf. Their terrace house was in Longport, a mile further down the valley than Burslem, in a street whose pavements were made of dark purple tiles. Pot-banks were all around. On foggy days breathing was like trying to inhale over a jug of Friar's Balsam, but in my aunt's house the grime was not allowed to settle. Sills were dusted. The kitchen table was scrubbed white. The radio, veneered in walnut, with a front fretted like a church window, was polished daily. In the small back garden my uncle grew dahlias and chrysanthemums. His tomatoes flourished. His roses swarmed over the party wall. When I visited them I glimpsed an abundance, not of possessions but of proper pride. It was hard-won and it was their due.

When my Uncle Ernest learned that I was being sent away to school he did not seem to me to be over-impressed. After my mother's operation he visited her on Wednesday evenings, walking up the long hill from his own home whatever the weather, and sinking into a seat by the fire, wordless until he had regained his breath. Always, he sat in the rocking chair, hitching up his trousers before lowering himself on to the green plush seat, then filling his pipe from a leather pouch, his fingers nimble and invisible as he crammed the bowl, his expression mildly sceptical as my mother retailed the latest bulletin of family news.

'And Hilda's having a dreadful time with her stomach,' she said. 'They've been doing overtime at the bank and it always plays her up. It's the hours, you know. She's like her father was. The slightest upset and she's poorly.'

My Uncle Ernest grunted and applied a match to his pipe, Hilda was my cousin, the daughter of Aunt Ada and Uncle Albert who had died the previous year. She dressed smartly and smoked cigarettes and her accent was smooth like the chrome rails on the chairs at the bank where she worked as a cashier. 'Has she tried senna pods?' he enquired.

My mother sighed. 'It's not that at all. You know very well. She's like Albert. She gets sick. She can't eat a morsel.'

'She would if she was hungry.'

'If it goes on Ada says she's keeping her at home,' said my mother. She had the extraordinary ability to absorb other people's information and attitudes and reproduce them without the slightest tinge of her own opinion. It was a kind of unconscious mimicry. House-bound, she had become a relay station for items of fact and gossip which she passed on to the next rider who would then continue the round. No one in the family owned a telephone, but the currency was swift. My mother was also the family correspondent, remembering birthdays and anniversaries as an act of love and duty, writing cards and letters, even to someone in the next avenue, because, as she often said, she felt it was her job 'to keep in touch'.

When it was first proposed that I should go away to school my Uncle Ernest was consulted, although he was not directly concerned in the mechanics of the operation. 'What dust tha' think on it?' he asked me, broadening his accent to the evident irritation of Uncle Percy, the headmaster of the local primary school, who was also paying us a visit that evening.

'He knows it's a great opportunity,' said my mother.

Uncle Ernest tickled my ribs. 'What dust tha' think, butcher?' His nicknames for me varied, but they all intimated that I was a terror, not to be trifled with. Sometimes he called me 'soldier', or 'admiral'. Other people found it confusing but I recognised the words as terms of endearment.

'I'd rather stay at home,' I said.

Uncle Percy polished his nose, a prominent feature of his raw-boned face. 'Too late I'm afraid. Much too late.'

'How's that?' enquired Uncle Ernest. 'He's not gone yet.'

'He soon will be.'

'Everyone's worked so hard to give him the chance,' said my mother.

Uncle Ernest lit his pipe again and sucked at it so vigorously that his face was completely masked by blue smoke. He beat it away and leaned forward. 'We know about chances,' he said. 'I've been hearing about chances since I was born. They're none so marvellous in themselves. They've got to be the right ones at the right time.' He removed his pipe from his mouth and a thread of spittle hung from the stem. 'I can see the sense of it. There's no denying it. But don't make the lad feel bound to be a champion. We can't all bring home a silver cup.'

'Some of us do,' said Uncle Percy, 'given the opportunity.'

My Uncle Ernest patted my cheek. 'Just do your best,' he said.

'That's all we ask,' said my mother.

Waiting outside Mr Gibbs's study I remembered what they had said. There were ten of us, all new boys, pressed against the wall of the corridor, our hair watered and combed, our shoes shined, our house ties carefully knotted. The headmaster's address, Mr Granger had advised us, would be brief. We would be told which forms we were to join, what rules we must especially heed, what penalties we would incur if the rules were broken. The door opened and Mr Gibbs looked out. 'Come,' he intoned.

We shuffled into the study and stood in a double line in front of the desk. Mr Gibbs looked us up and down as if we were troops on parade. 'You,' he said to Minton, who stood beside me, 'your hair's like a girl's. Get it cut.' He studied my shoes. 'A decent shine,' he said, 'but untidy laces. Learn to tie them properly.' He inserted his finger into the collar band of the boy at the end of the front rank and peered distastefully into the gap between the shirt and his neck. 'Filthy,' he declared. 'Go and wash it when you leave this study, then report back to me.' He swung round and indicated the wall behind his desk where canes of various lengths and thicknesses hung on small brass hooks. 'These are my adjutants,' said Mr Gibbs. 'They make sure that my rules are carried out. I do not like to send them into action. But if we are in disagreement, I will. Believe me, I will.'

As Mr Granger had forecast we were given a resumé of the rules and what would befall us if we transgressed. The briefing was short but comprehensive and it seemed to me that actual lessons played only a small part in the curriculum. Each boy's scholastic record was reviewed and I was assigned to Form 1B. 'B forms,' said Mr Gibbs 'are for boys who have the ability to succeed, but have hitherto lacked the will. In placing you in such a form I may be misjudging you, but it is your job to prove me wrong. I hope that you do.' He pushed his chair back so that the castors squealed. 'One more point,' he said, 'how many of you have been circumcised?'

Three boys put up their hands. The rest of us hesitated and Mr Gibbs frowned impatiently. 'Circumcision is an operation performed on your private parts. Your penis, in point of fact. If your foreskin is too tight it is removed surgically.' He scanned our faces and frowned more severely. 'Is there any one of you who does not understand me?' I watched Minton nervously raise his hand again and I followed his example. Mr Gibbs leaned across his desk. 'Exactly what is it you do not understand?'

'The words, sir,' said Minton.

'Which words?'

'All of them, sir.'

'How old are you, boy?' asked Mr Gibbs.

'Nine, sir.'

'And you?'

'Eight,' I said.

'And no one, not even your religious instructors, has explained these words to you before?'

We shook our heads. I felt my face and my ears burning. The mention of religion introduced yet another confusing element into the discussion. I felt frightened and embarrassed. What could an operation on my private parts have to do with singing hymns in our pew at Hill Top? How did it relate to my father explaining the story of the ears of corn? 'I am amazed,' said Mr Gibbs. 'I cannot blame you. Education of this sort is not your responsibility. But it astounds me that no one has thought fit to instruct you in such elementary matters of sexual hygiene.' He then repaired the omission in some detail, drawing on his years as a teacher and his time in the trenches, where, he said ominously, sexual ignorance and neglect has caused as many casualties as shell-fire. 'Circumcision,' he said finally, 'was first practised by the Jews. But that fact should not blind us to its benefits.' My confusion was now complete. I confessed that my foreskin was still intact and stumbled out of Mr Gibbs's office in a daze.

'What did he mean about the Jews?' I asked Minton.

'You heard him,' he said, 'they started it.'

'Snip, snip,' said Fisher. 'Yiddisher scissors.'

I had never, as far as I was aware, met a Jew. I recognised them in comics of course; generally fat, hook-nosed and wearing diamond rings. They were interested in money – a characteristic shared by several members of my own family. But they were also sharp. Money stuck to them. I remembered Aunt Ada telling how she had argued over the price of a blouse made by a Jewish dressmaker, rubbing her fingers and thumb together as she described the hard bargain that had been struck. Unless you took care, I understood, Jews got the better of you. They were also vulgar. Uncle Frank, my most-travelled relation who had built roads on the Gold Coast and been photographed in America with J. Edgar Hoover, wrote to my mother regretting the fact that he had bought a bungalow at Westcliff-on Sea because of its proximity to Southend. It was, he said, the new Jerusalem. Jews were, of course, artistically talented like black people and, in the same way, their art excused them the worst characteristics of their race. We admired Solomon the pianist and laughed at the jokes of Issy Bonn.

He was broad, said my mother, but her eyes dimmed when he sang My Yiddisher Momma. I remember seeing his photograph in the Radio Times: a smiling, thick-set man, with his hat pushed to the back of his head. His exuberance seemed to lift the picture from the page as if it was embossed. But his vitality was alien. I sensed a strangeness. I acknowledged the difference.

There were also darker legends about the butchery of babies and the kidnapping of Christian maidens for reasons which were never made clear. They were stories not to be taken as evidence, but as grounds for suspicion, rather as *The Story of Maria Monk* – on sale in the local newsagents, with its cover illustration of a sorrowful nun menaced by lowering convent walls – was regarded as a lurid, but most likely accurate account of popish goings-on which had leaked out despite the attempts of Catholics to keep it secret.

'Not half,' said Fisher. 'I had mine bandaged for three weeks. I was off school for a month.'

'Did you see the doctor do it?' I asked.

Fisher rolled his eyes despairingly. 'Course I didn't. They gave me gas. When I woke up it was all done. They don't let you watch things like that.'

'What does it look like now?' asked Minton.

'Show us,' I said.

We hurried to the lavatories on the far side of the quadrangle and crowded into a cubicle. Fisher unbuttoned his fly and took out his penis. It lay in the palm of his hand like a small sausage roll with the meat slightly protruding from the pastry. We studied it for several seconds. Minton touched it gingerly. 'Does it still hurt?'

'Not any more.'

Minton and I also undid our buttons and pulled out our penises. 'Mine's biggest,' said Fisher. It was undoubtedly true. 'I can make it bigger,' he boasted.

There were footsteps outside and someone rattled the door. 'What's going on in there?'

We hastily did up our buttons and I lifted the latch. 'Just talking,' I said.

'Talking?' It was one of the senior boys who wore a

prefect's badge in the lapel of his blazer. 'You weren't just talking,' he said. 'You were up to something filthy.'

'We weren't,' said Fisher. 'Honestly. We were sharing these out.' He produced a tube of fruit gums. 'We didn't want the others to see.'

Almost absent-mindedly the prefect took possession of the gums. 'You were pulling pudding,' he said. 'That's what I think. You'll go blind. You know that don't you?' He stepped back and waved us out of the cubicle. 'Cut along to class and don't let me catch you here again.' He watched us scuttle across the quadrangle, his fingers already peeling the foil from the roll of gums. 'I remember your faces,' he called. 'I'll be watching for you.'

Around the bend of the corridor we paused to recover our breath. 'Greedy pig,' said Fisher, 'he just pinched those gums. We ought to report him.'

'Then he'll tell on us,' said Minton.

'He's got nothing to tell.'

'He'll make something up,' I said. 'Anyway, we don't know his name.'

We savoured the heady mixture of injustice and relief, a sensation with which I was to become familiar. For a moment I saw myself suspended outside my own body, seeing our three figures – like cartoon sketches – huddled together in the corridor, consumed and overwhelmed by the mass of the school. It seemed capable of digesting us, absorbing every trace of our bodies and identities. I did not find it frightening but inevitable, a state of affairs about which we could grumble but which we had to accept. The machinery of the school, the system by which it operated was still largely unknown, but I sensed hidden wheels revolving in the dark, doors swinging open on great hinges and closing on chambers in which councils deliberated and decisions were made. It was the image of a tradition to which, I realised, we now belonged. 'Forget about the fruit gums,' I said, 'we're supposed to be in class.'

We arrived ten minutes after the others had been marked present. Our form master, I discovered, was Mr Smith and he was displeased by our late arrival. 'You what!' he said incredulously. 'You went to be relieved! When you are sent to your classroom by the headmaster you proceed in a straight line, the shortest route from A to B.' He put his hands on his hips and stooped forward until our eyes were level. 'That is a definition I advise you to learn by heart.' He picked up a ruler from his desk and swished it through the air. 'This should help you remember. Hold out your right hands.' He delivered three strokes each with the flat of the ruler, choosing the point of impact as carefully as a batsman marking out his crease. 'Right then,' he said. 'That's that. Welcome to Form 1B.'

Five

MR SMITH was in charge of Form 1B, claimed Carpenter, because, academically speaking, he was a fool. Carpenter, who was two years older than me, was in Form 2B but he had spent the previous year being supervised by Mr Smith and he spoke from experience. It was not only his teaching he despised. 'Just listen to him talk,' he said, 'you can't help laughing.'

Mr Smith's way of speaking, as I had noticed when we first met, was unusual. It was flat and emphatic, one word following another like coping stones being dropped on to a wet bed of cement. His sentences were sway-backed and sagged in the middle but their meaning was still adamant. He did not exaggerate accent and idiom as my Uncle Ernest sometimes did to colour an anecdote or annoy an adversary. His speech was naturally graceless. His words were pitched together as though he resented having to use them. He regarded conversation as effete; a poor substitute for action.

For a while, though, he taught us English. He took no chances with grammar, most likely because he saw nouns, verbs and adjectives as natural enemies and his one attempt to demonstrate the use of different tenses was a forlorn adventure which left us all more mystified than when we began. His answer to the problem was to set us essays to write. The subjects were beautifully simple: My Favourite Pet, My Favourite Sport, My Best Holiday, What I Want to Be When I Am a Man. He insisted that we filled four pages in our exercise books and, what was equally important, that we maintained complete silence while writing. It was essential for us to concentrate, he said. But sometimes the calm was broken by the sound of Mr Smith's heavy breathing, a stertorous rasp which issued from his open mouth as he sat with his chair tilted backwards, his feet braced against the centre strut of his desk and the daily paper spread across his lap.

He justified the paper by using it as his crib during Current Affairs quizzes, which did not actually appear on the syllabus but which Mr Smith would announce, usually towards the end of another class when time was dragging and the interval bell was unaccountably delayed. The questions he asked were not profound, but he would sometimes prime them with undeclared booby-traps.

'Who's the King of Abyssinia?' he would enquire.

'Haile Selassie, sir.'

'No he's not.'

'Yes he is, sir.'

'Are you certain?'

'Yes sir.'

'Positive?'

'Yes sir.'

'Tell him why he's wrong, Oakes.'

'He's not the King, sir. He's the Emperor.'

'Correct.' Mr Smith tapped his red, ridged forehead with his index finger. 'It's not how much brain you've got that matters. It's how you use it.' He nodded gravely as if he was imparting a vital secret. 'Putting the grey matter to work. That's the trick.' It was a question of discipline, he said. 'Mental fitness is like physical fitness,' he declared. 'You need to take the proper exercise. Keep on your toes. Think fast. Develop your reflexes.'

He asked us sporting questions, few of which I could answer except those which dealt with boxing. Tiny Bostock, the British flyweight champion, had once been my cousin Jessie's office boy and following his career had been a matter of local pride which I learned to adapt as expertise. I scored a remarkable success by reeling off the official poundage of bantamweights to heavyweights and set the seal on my triumph by tossing in the information that light-heavies were also known as cruiserweights. Even Mr Smith was impressed, but his approval raised my self-confidence to a dangerous level. The reckoning came during an English lesson for which we had written an essay on the theme of My Favourite Book. I had chosen *Tarzan of the Apes*, partly because it struck me as a more sophisticated title than the school stories of Gunby Hadath and Talbot Baines Reed which I knew my class-mates would opt for but also because it seemed likely that Mr Smith, whose knowledge of literature was limited, might have encountered the Ape Man in the cinema if not in print. I had guessed rightly, but my reflexes were too fast. I had been too clever by half.

Mr Smith read my essay with a frown which grew sterner with each successive line. Several times he shook his head as if trying to clear water from his ears. He turned back a page and read it again. It was difficult to decide whether he was engrossed or simply baffled. Eventually he beckoned me to his desk. 'There's something wrong here,' he said.

'What's that, sir?'

'It's the names,' he said. 'You've got them back to front.'

I was bewildered. My recollection of Tarzan's jungle birth, the death of his parents Lord and Lady Greystoke and his adoption by the tribe of wild apes was absolutely clear. At home I had built up my own toy menagerie and named them after the principal characters in the book. There was Kerchak the bull ape; Kala his mate, who had mothered the infant Tarzan; Tantor the elephant, Sabor the lioness; Horta the boar and Bolgani the gorilla. I knew their names as well as I knew my own. 'How have I got them wrong, sir?' I asked.

Mr Smith folded his hands on the desk top. 'Try and think of them as people,' he said patiently. 'Think of how they're called. Take your own name for instance. How is it made up?'

I studied his crimson face with its bleached eyebrows and lid of golden hair but I saw no clue to the answer he sought. Brylcreem glistened on his scalp and a scrap of tissue paper glared from a nick he had made on his chin while shaving. I sensed that behind his slightly bloodshot eyes a transmitter was hammering out a message I was unable to read and that with every second its signal was becoming more exasperated. 'I've got three names, sir,' I said.

'Three?'

'Philip Barlow Oakes,' I said. 'My Christian name, my mother's maiden name and my surname.'

'Forget the middle name,' said Mr Smith. 'That complicates things. Concentrate on your Christian name and your surname. Right. Have we got that straight? Now think of the animals. They're like people, aren't they?'

'Sort of,' I said doubtfully.

Mr Smith flexed his fingers until his knuckles cracked. 'They're like people,' he said. 'There's no doubt about it. That's what the author meant. And he's given them names like proper people.' He paused, evidently expecting me to grasp the logic of his argument. When I still hesitated he scowled. 'Don't be daft,' he said. 'It's perfectly plain. It's not Kala *the* ape. It's Kala Ape. It's not Sabor *the* lioness. It's Sabor Lioness. Christian name and surname.' He plucked the scrap of paper from his chin and a bead of blood instantly welled up. 'Do you understand what I'm saying?'

I swallowed hard. 'I think so.'

'I should hope you do. It's only commonsense. You've got it in children's stories. Look at Peter Rabbit. And in nursery rhymes. Look at Baa-baa Blacksheep. This is the same.' He handed me back my exercise book. 'Write it out again.'

'All of it, sir?'

'All of it. So you'll remember.'

The art of being taught by Mr Smith demanded a special kind of collaboration, but it took me months to learn. It was true that he was Mrs Gibbs's cousin, which explained why he had been taken on the staff. But he seemed to resent the appointment and often I would see him in mid-class staring through the window like a prisoner yearning for his freedom. At other times he would project a vigour that flickered around him like an electric halo, banishing the demons of lassitude. He strode down corridors swinging his arms like clubs, holding himself so stiffly that a plank could have been nailed between the nape of his neck and the crocodile belt which supported his slacks. His energy would have fired a locomotive, but it was desperate. It was harnessed to nothing. Its purpose was to consume itself.

As a famous cricketer – whose fame, we slowly realised, was on the wane – Mr Smith was sometimes invited to sporting dinners. His preparations were elaborate. At seven-thirty he would swagger through the dormitory to the staff bathroom, a cravat knotted around his throat, a silk handkerchief trailing from the breast pocket of his silk dressing gown. Half an hour later he would emerge, his face and hair newly burnished, a towel slung over one shoulder. At eight o'clock, as his taxi crunched up the gravel drive, he would step from his cabin, uniformed in evening dress. Invariably he would check the contents of his wallet, make sure that his cigarette case was full, that his lighter worked and that his shirt studs were all in place before he marched off into the night, leaving in his wake the leathery tang of cologne. At the dinner he made a speech. From the accounts we read in the local paper it always seemed to be the same speech, peppered with complaints about the selectors, body-line bowling and the unpredictable state of the wicket. Mr Smith was a purist about wickets. In months to come I was to spend hours, yoked in tandem with one of my fellow juniors, hauling a heavy roller over the newly mown pitch. It was not punishment, Mr Smith insisted; it was part of the game.

His return from the dinner could follow one of two courses. If it had been a success ('Remarks by Mr Frank Smith were warmly applauded') he would proceed in a fairly straight line down the middle of the dormitory and disappear into his cabin without further incident. If he felt he had been slighted or that his expert knowledge had fallen on heedless ears he would take reprisals. Instead of making directly to his cabin down the centre aisle he would walk slowly and stiff-legged along the narrow alley between the wall and our bed-heads. A hot water pipe which linked the radiators ran along the skirting board. It was used by radio enthusiasts as the earth for their crystal sets and Mr Smith's progress – his feet and shin-bones acting like flails – severed every wire, striking head-phones dumb as he marched grimly on. Radios in the dormitory were forbidden and he could easily have confiscated the lot. He chose never to mention them. When Mr Smith was held in proper esteem we listened to Carroll Gibbons and Lew Stone without interruption. The axe fell only when he was denied his due.

He had an acute sense of what was deserved, what was appropriate. He accepted the distinction between gentlemen and players, but in no way did he regard himself as anyone's inferior. He was a professional, a man apart and he dressed accordingly. For a start, he owned more suits than any other member of the staff. For church services he wore a grey bird's-eye worsted with a navy-blue tie. He had at least four sports jackets, checked and hound's-tooth, all with leather buttons. He had a trench-coat whose belt was fringed with small brass loops, designed – we were told – to carry hand grenades. He had a blue Melton overcoat and another of brown Harris tweed. He had a dazzling selection of silk handkerchiefs and scarves, mostly striped and spotted, and his shirts were all monogrammed on the breast pocket. For cricket he wore white, with a thick cable-stitched sweater whose cuffs and neckline were embroidered in red and gold. His cap was ringed with the same colours and fitted his head as snugly as his hair. His wrist-watch was gold and he wore a gold ring with a red stone on the little finger of his right hand.

On four days a week he took us for Physical Training, streamlined in his singlet, slacks and running shoes – an almost luminous figure in the green-painted gymnasium with its bald vaulting horse and scuffed floor. Ropes dangled from the steel beams spanning the roof and there were piles of coconut matting in each corner, their edges crimped like old sticking plasters. The floor boomed beneath our feet as if we were dancing on a drum. In the summer term the boards came up and the gym became a swimming pool. But on dry land Mr Smith was our mentor and his methods were spartan.

On winter mornings when the air itself seemed furred with frost he began the lesson with a jog round the school playing fields. The small side gate in the playground was unlocked and in single file we trotted across the main road, pimpled with cold, the scars on our knees and knuckles turning a paler shade of blue than our gym shorts. Mr Smith pranced alongside the column, his head held high, his fists jerking like pistons across his chest. 'On your toes!' he shouted. 'Stop plodding!' We made three circuits of the lower field, tripping on mole hills, feeling the ice in small puddles splinter beneath our feet. I saw cobwebs in the hedges like stars which had frozen the moment they exploded. Blackbirds scanned us with bright yellow eyes before darting explosively for cover. On the pavement flanking the field people stood watching us.

We maintained our own orbit, Mr Smith sprinting beside us, harrying those at the rear, urging the leaders to step up the pace. Breathing was like gulping an iron pillow. My nose streamed on to my upper lip and I licked it dry. Steam hung over us as if we had stepped from a bath. We completed the third circuit and staggered back to the school, Mr Smith still beside us bawling instructions, warning us to stay on our toes, to keep moving, to look lively. 'All right,' he said when we reached the gym, 'you can take a breather.' It was for no longer than thirty seconds. After that we did physical jerks, we vaulted the horse, we climbed the ropes and we turned somersaults on the mats. 'Now,' said Mr Smith, 'everyone in the showers.'

To begin with the water was reasonably warm, but without warning Mr Smith would switch it to cold and there would be a rush for the towels heaped on the slatted bench. Mr Smith stood in the middle of the room watching us trying to scrub heat back into our bodies. 'D'you know what nesh is?' he demanded. 'Nesh means soft and that's what you are. We're going to change that. We're going to toughen you up. We're going to make iron men of you.' Sometimes while he made his speech he practised running on the spot, proving that he was as good as his word, setting an example to us all. I did not think of him as being made of iron; his colouring was too vivid. He reminded me of steak being weighed on brass scales, the meat and the metal both radiant.

Mr Smith did not teach boxing. It was not a compulsory sport but a club activity run by the senior mathematics master, Mr Pope, who dressed for the part in baggy trousers and a roll-necked sweater like a sparring partner in an American B movie. He had short, curly grey hair. His mouth gaped like a turbot as if he had difficulty in breathing through his nose and his expression was unfailingly benign even when he was demonstrating combination punches which were designed to tear an opponent's head off. Boxing, for him, was a sweet science although he did not have anything like the physique of a fighter. His arms and legs were too short. His feet were flat and his chest merged with his belly into a barrel of firm blubber. Boxing, he emphasised, was the art of self-defence and to prove it he invited Ted 'Kid' Lewis, once the holder of three British titles, to visit the school.

The Kid held court in the gymnasium. He removed his jacket, revealing a striped shirt with gilt armbands hoisting up the sleeves and put on a pair of boxing gloves. 'What I want to show you,' he said, 'is how to stay out of trouble.' He pointed to a spot in the centre of the ring and planted his feet, natty in patent leather, on either side of it. 'I won't move from here,' he said. 'What I want you to do is try and hit me. One at a time, that is. Anyone who lands a punch gets half a dollar.'

Carpenter was first in line. 'You won't hit me back?' he asked.

The Kid shook his head. 'I won't touch you son.'

Carpenter aimed a straight left and the Kid leaned back so that the punch landed short. Carpenter swung a right cross and the Kid swayed to one side; a left cross and he swayed the other way. He ducked, he bobbed, he weaved and he feinted and at the end of a minute Carpenter was red-faced and out of breath.

Mr Pope rang the time-keeper's bell, a shell-case brought back from the trenches by the headmaster. 'Next man in the ring,' he called.

The performance was repeated a dozen times. Beneath the single lamp burning down on the grubby canvas Kid Lewis remained immaculate. Not a hair of his head was ruffled, not a drop of sweat appeared on his brow. He cheerfully avoided every assault, signed autographs, shook hands all round and became our hero. 'Mind you,' he said as he shrugged back into his jacket, 'I had to learn the hard way. It's no fun getting hurt.'

The only person who was not enthusiastic about the display was Mr Smith. The next day he spent half the

English lesson explaining why attack was a far superior form of defence than that demonstrated by Kid Lewis. 'Look at the real champions,' he said. 'They've all got the killer instinct. They don't mind taking a bit of punishment on the way. Take Dempsey. Take Schmeling. They're not bothered about their pretty faces. They don't waste time dodging all over the shop. They know what they have to do. Get in there and finish the other man off. That's what it's all about.' He paused meaningfully. 'Mind you, they have the advantage. They have the temperament. They're not Jew-boys.'

Minton put up his hand. 'Is Mr Lewis?'

Mr Smith leaned against his desk and jingled the coins in his trouser pockets. 'Oh yes,' he said. 'I think it's fairly common knowledge that Mr Lewis is one of the chosen race. I don't think he'd deny that. There are plenty of Hebrew gentlemen in boxing. They've made it a very nice business. Not like cricket. There's no profit in that.' He stopped abruptly as if aware that he had opened a door marked 'Private'. 'Any road,' he said 'we're not here to talk about Mr Lewis. There's twenty minutes to the bell. We'll have a spot of reading.'

Later I told Carpenter what Mr Smith had said. He was not surprised. 'He's always going on about Ikey Moe.'

'Ikey Moe?'

'Jew-boys. The Yids. He used to tell us we could be proud of this school for one thing if nothing else. We've got none of them here. It's in the rules.' He ran his finger down an imaginary page. 'All boys will receive a Christian education. That's what it means.'

'I see,' I said untruthfully.

'Mind you,' said Carpenter, 'Vic thinks it's all wrong. He says it's got to change.' He screwed his finger against the side of his head in the gesture that I remembered. 'Loony,' he said. 'Proper loony.'

Vic was Mr Sleath who taught art and woodwork. He was a stout, garrulous man whose most remarkable feature was his nose, a bright purple bulb whose bridge was deeply indented by the wire frame of his spectacles. He took the initiative by drawing our attention to it when we assembled for our first lesson. 'All right,' he said, 'let's get it over with. What a conk. What a beauty.' He shook out his handkerchief and polished the tip so that it shone like an aubergine. 'Is it a boozer's nose?' he demanded rhetorically. 'No it is not. My nose happens to be this colour because I have a digestive disorder. The only alcohol which passes my lips is a glass of beer which I take with the headmaster on the last day of term. Nothing stronger and at no other time.'

In the army he had served as the headmaster's sergeant. 'Mr Gibbs was a major then,' he said. 'A fine officer. When he took up this appointment he invited me to come with him. And I did and I've never regretted it.' Behind him stood a stove on which a pot of glue simmered in a double boiler. In one corner there was a printing press. Lengths of timber lay in racks beside it. Unlike the rest of the school the scale of things seemed normal, domesticated. 'What I like,' said Mr Sleath, 'is a nice, snug place to work in. A good billet means good results.' He had a cottage close to the school where he lived with his wife and son, but the woodwork room – a long, single-storey shed, approached through the vegetable garden – was clearly where he felt most at home. 'You can always come and talk to me here,' he said. 'I know you'll have problems, things you don't want to bother the headmaster with. That's where I come in. I'm the one who listens.' He dusted his nose again, heightening the gloss. 'I'm not suggesting that you sneak. Far from it. Nobody loves a sneak. But there have been incidents – in the past, mind you – when I've been able to help. A word to the wise and so on. Sometimes it's better that way. Unofficial. I know how it is with new boys. It's not always easy. There are people who take advantage. Bigger boys I mean. In the dormitories, for instance. I know what goes on there. I've heard it all before.'

He was planing a piece of wood as he spoke and each sentence was measured by the sweep of the blade. The shavings curled crisply away from the block and fell at his feet. It was comforting to watch him at work. He was a homely man engaged in a homely task. The plane whispered over the wood, following the grain, closing in on the final shape. 'Anything you tell me will be in confidence,' said Mr Sleath. 'Just between you and me. Strictly private.'

The invitation to confide in him was bewildering. There was nothing which came immediately to mind which seemed to be of interest. His reference to bigger boys in the dormitories struck a faint chord, but it was hard to decide whether it was worth mentioning. On my second night at the school, long after lights out, the seniors had come to bed and one of them had stroked my cheek and asked if I was asleep.

'You woke me up,' I said.

'Were you dreaming?'

'I don't think so,' I said.

'Do you want to talk?'

'I don't mind.'

'Do you have any friends here?'

'Not really,' I said. 'Not yet. I know Carpenter, that's all.'

'My name's Tucker,' he said. He sat down on my bed and combed my hair with his fingers. 'Are you lonely?'

'A bit.'

'You don't have to be lonely. You could have a lot of friends.' His hand slid down the front of my night-shirt. 'Do you want a cuddle?' he whispered.

'With you?'

'Yes, with me.'

'Not really,' I said.

He withdrew his hand. 'All right then. Not if you don't want to,' he said. 'It's not important. It's just that I thought you might be homesick.'

I yawned loudly and he stood up. 'Go to sleep,' he said. 'I'll see you another time.' I heard him move away and when I next opened my eyes it was morning.

It was hardly worth describing the incident to Mr Sleath, I thought. No one had taken advantage of me. All that had happened was that Tucker had woken me up. He had even apologised. 'Sorry I disturbed you,' he said as I brushed my teeth in the ablutions the next day. Since then he had smiled at me in the dining hall and when we passed in the corridor but we had not exchanged another word. I decided to wait until something more disturbing happened before I told Mr Sleath.

Meanwhile, his own confessions multiplied. 'There's something else about me that you should know,' he said. 'I bear witness to the Lord. I praise His Name. I testify to His greatness.' He removed the block of wood he had been planing from the vice and stroked the new edge with his index finger. 'That surprised you, didn't it?' he said. 'It surprises a lot of people. It amuses them too. I get laughed at. But I glory in it. My Redeemer liveth and I proclaim the fact. Each Saturday night I go to Birmingham, to the Bullring and I tell the people. I have a little stand there and I read from the Holy Bible and I say a few prayers and I praise the Lord.' He took off his glasses and polished them on the end of his tie. Unprotected, his eyes looked small and mad and sore.

'I told the headmaster what I proposed to do,' he said. 'In fact, it was when we were serving together in France that I knew I had to serve my Maker. I had been given my life, redeemed twice over and I knew that forever more I was His servant. "I have to do this thing, sir," I said. And he said "Very well, Sleath. No one should stand between a man and his God". And I went and did it and no matter how much people have mocked he has never told me I was bringing the school into disrepute and I admire him for that.' He stood silent for a while with his head bowed as if he was praying, then he seemed to gather strength.

'It's a calling really,' he said. 'It cannot be denied. I am but a voice crying in the wilderness, but one day my seed may fall on fertile ground. The time is approaching when the truth will be known. The historical truth, I mean. The Lost Tribe will return to the fold. The British Israelites will return to the true faith.' His voice was shrill. His spectacles were jerking so violently in his hand that one of the arms swung loose. He noticed it in time and tightened the screw before putting the glasses back on. Normality was restored. He glanced at the glue pot as if to remind himself where we were. He smiled without embarrassment.

'Words,' he said. 'I may go on a bit, but I mean what I say. Take nicknames. Officially, I'm Mr Sleath but I know that most of you call me Vic. Not to my face, mind. But it's friendly. It's what a nickname should be. In fact, the only words I object to are blasphemies. Thou shalt not take the name of the Lord thy God in vain. Remember that. Even by accident. I never want to hear anyone saying "Gorblimey". Never. What you are saying is "God blind me" and believe me, He will! No request goes unanswered. Bear that in mind.' Across the gardens a bell rang signalling the end of the period. Mr Sleath spread his hands dismissing us.

We walked past the plantation of Brussels sprouts and the potato clamp where starlings foraged. 'What was all that about?' demanded Minton.

I screwed my finger against my temple. 'Loony,' I said.

Six

DURING THE WEEK our blue cloaks hung in a long wardrobe with sliding doors in the dormitory nearest to the sewing room. It was a favourite hiding place in games of hide and seek. The doors could be pulled shut from inside the wardrobe, but it was important to remember to stick a pencil between the door and the jamb so that the catch would not engage, leaving us trapped between layers of serge, choking on dust and camphor. Once, it was rumoured, a boy had been found dead in the wardrobe, his nails broken and bloody from his attempts to wrench the door open. We added his ghost to those which already haunted the school: John Lees, the founder; a kitchen-maid who had drowned in a vat of porridge; a school porter, a veteran of the Crimean War, who was seen on winter nights limping up the stairs to the clock tower.

Darkness added spice to our games. We could trespass unseen, plunder without being detected. Squatting on the hot-water pipes in the dormitory, we invented dares, egging each other on to wilder, more scary feats of recklessness. The previous term, said Carpenter, one boy had climbed on to the school roof at midnight, leaving a pair of underpants impaled on the lightning conductor. Another had crept into the headmaster's study and sawn half-way through his largest cane with a fretwork blade. In each case the investigations had been exhaustive but no culprit had been found.

'What about pinching Smithy's best scarf,' suggested Burton.

Carpenter shook his head. 'Too close to home.'

'How about filling the ink-wells with carbide,' proposed Fisher.

Carpenter shook his head again. 'They only fizz when

you pour the ink in on top.' He poked me in the ribs. 'Are you feeling hungry?'

'A bit peckish,' I said.

Carpenter put his arm round my shoulder. 'There's masses of stuff in the kitchens. Why don't we take a look.'

'Have you done it before?'

'Hundreds of times,' he said. 'How d'you fancy some slab cake or a few biscuits. They've got Garibaldis. I saw them this morning.'

'You wouldn't dare,' said Burton.

Carpenter hauled me to my feet. 'Come on,' he said. 'You and me. Let's do it.'

The kitchens lay to the rear of the school separating us from the girls' wing. After tea the serving tables were scrubbed and the floors swabbed down. By eight o'clock they were usually deserted, damp and cavernous, smelling of mould and scouring powder. Giant saucepans and trays were stacked on the dressers like armour awaiting the next day's tourney. There was a huge corrugated drum, big enough for a small boy to stand in, which was turned with a handle to rasp the skin off tons of potatoes. Inside the meat safe carcases of sheep, split like kindling, dangled in rows, the frost glinting on kidneys that ogled from their ruptured envelopes of fat.

There was a night staff of two or three maids who began preparations for breakfast the next day and made bed-time drinks and sandwiches for masters who requested them. But they worked in a small annexe, the door to which was usually closed. Their radio, tuned to Luxembourg, was played at full blast and they sang along with the bands. As we crept into the main kitchen, hugging the shadows, we heard them harmonising on Red Sails in the Sunset and I'll String Along with You. Two of them began to dance, their shadows flowing like water along the gap at the bottom of the door.

'I may not be an angel,' sang one of them and the other giggled.

Carpenter pointed to the far side of the kitchen. 'The store cupboard's over there,' he hissed. 'That's where they keep the cake and stuff.'

Without warning the door to the annexe opened and we pressed ourselves to the wall as one of the girls crossed the room and filled a kettle at the sink. My bladder winced sympathetically at the sound of running water. I squirmed in discomfort and Carpenter gave me a warning nudge. The maid stood with her back to us, one foot still beating time to the music. 'I learned the chassé last week,' she called. 'Forward and reverse.' She turned off the tap and danced across the kitchen, demonstrating the step. Half-way across the room she saw us. 'My God!' she said. 'Burglars!'

I froze where I was, but Carpenter stepped into the light. 'We're not burglars,' he said. He nodded towards her feet. 'I can do that,' he said. 'My sister taught me.'

The maid put the kettle down on the serving table that ran the length of the room. 'And what else did she teach you? How to pinch things that don't belong to you?'

One of the other girls came to the door of the annexe. 'What's up, Doris?'

'We've got visitors,' she said. 'Charley Peace and Bill Sykes.' She picked up the kettle and motioned us forward. 'Let's have a look at you. Quick march.'

I followed Carpenter into the annexe with Doris bringing up the rear. She closed the door behind us. 'Proper villains,' she said, 'you can tell.' She tapped me under the chin. 'What are you doing here?'

'We were hungry,' said Carpenter.

'Hungry?'

'We missed tea,' said Carpenter. 'We were in detention.'

Doris put the kettle on the stove and lit the gas. 'Were you now? For being bad boys. What d'you reckon Betty? What should we do with them Pearl?'

The music still played and Carpenter made a small bow. 'May I have the pleasure?' he said.

'Cheeky devil,' said Doris.

'I can do the feather step as well,' said Carpenter.

'Even in your night-shirt?' said Betty.

Carpenter looked hang-dog: 'Even when I'm starving.' He put his arm round Doris's waist and clasped her left hand. They moved together as one, spinning smartly round the room, their feet whisking over the tiles as if they were on a cushion of air. The tune came to an end and Carpenter stepped back and repeated his bow.

'Cheeky devil,' said Doris again. She leaned against the stove and looked us up and down. 'How old are you?'

'Nearly eleven,' said Carpenter.

'Eight,' I said.

Doris nodded solemnly. 'He's leading you into evil ways. You know that don't you?'

'Not really,' I said.

'Wicked,' said Doris. 'Leading you astray.' She turned to Carpenter. 'You say your sister taught you how to dance? Not your girl friend?'

'Have you got a girl friend?' asked Pearl.

'Course he has,' said Betty. 'What's her name?'

Carpenter took his time. The kettle began to boil and a plume of steam like an ostrich feather quivered in the air. He looked at them each in turn. 'It's Doris,' he said.

Pearl bit her lip, suppressing a smile. 'You're right,' she said. 'He is a cheeky devil and no mistake.'

'Does she look like me?' asked Doris. She was about fifteen, I guessed, slightly built with wavy auburn hair on which her maid's cap rested like the trimming of a Christmas cake.

'You're prettier,' said Carpenter.

'What d'you do with her,' asked Betty. 'Do you kiss her?'

Carpenter studied the floor, then glanced up through his lashes. He brushed aside a lock of black hair and smiled modestly. 'Sometimes.'

'What else do you do?' demanded Pearl.

'Nothing.'

'You're a big boy,' said Betty. 'Big for your age.'

'Not big enough for that,' said Doris. She wagged her finger at us like a baton. 'Listen,' she said, 'you can have a cup of tea, then it's back to bed. And don't get caught, else we'll be in trouble. We've enough of that already.' She cut us a slice of cake each and filled a bag with broken biscuits. 'You can take these with you. And think yourselves lucky.'

Carpenter studied her over the rim of his cup. 'Do you have a boy friend?'

She slapped his wrist, but not hard enough to sting. 'None of your business.'

'He's keen,' said Betty. 'I told you.'

'He's so sharp he'll cut himself,' said Pearl.

'If you have,' said Carpenter, 'he's the lucky one.'

Along the corridor a door opened and closed. Doris snatched up our cups and hid them behind a bread bin. 'Off you go,' she said, 'and take care.'

Carpenter hesitated for a moment then reached up and kissed her on the lips. 'Abyssinia,' he said.

We scuttled through the kitchen, across the quadrangle and up the back stairs. Night-lights glowed high in the dormitory ceiling. In the distance a lavatory flushed. There was no light in Mr Smith's cabin, but it was too early for him to come to bed yet. We reached our own beds and stripped down to our night-shirts. Carpenter shook Burton awake. 'Have a biscuit,' he said. 'Compliments of the kitchen.'

We sat on the hot pipe behind Carpenter's bed and shared his radio headphones. Roy Fox played Smoke Gets in Your Eyes and I imagined the girls in the annexe dancing to the music – Pearl leading, Doris lying back in her arms, her eyes half-closed, her teeth gleaming between her parted lips. 'What was it like kissing her?' I asked.

Carpenter broke a biscuit into small pieces and nibbled them one after the other. 'She had lipstick on,' he said finally. 'I can still taste it.'

'Was it true about having a girl friend?'

I felt him shake with laughter. 'Course not. I was having them on.'

'They're nice,' I said.

Carpenter handed me a final biscuit, then tucked the bag under his pillow. 'Nice enough,' he said, 'for skivvies.'

It was a word which the headmaster had forbidden us to use. It was abusive and archaic he said and the staff objected. They had, in fact, called on him to say so. Their delegation was led by the cook, an immense woman, whose white expanse of uniform seemed to cry out for medals or a coloured sash and whose mighty arms were pocked by dimples at each elbow. 'Skivvy,' said Mr Gibbs 'is a derogatory term. The ladies who cook and clean for you object to being so described. And I agree. There is no reason in the world why they should put up with your bad manners. I have asked them to report any boy who offends in this way. And I promise you that his discourtesy will be punished.' He folded his arms on the assembly hall Bible as if his entire body was taking a vow and glared at us through his rimless glasses.

'Gibbo said we weren't to use that word,' I reminded Carpenter. 'He said it was insulting.'

'I'm not insulting anybody. Skivvies are skivvies. That's all I said.'

'You said they were nice enough.'

'So they are. They're just different.'

'Who from?'

'Me,' said Carpenter. 'You. Gibbo. There's nothing wrong with them. I'm not saying that. They're just different.' He grabbed my arm to emphasise the point. 'Look,' he said 'does anyone in your family go out to scrub floors?'

I shook my head. 'We have someone to do it.'

'That's what I mean.'

'But she's not a skivvy,' I said. 'She's our housekeeper. She lives with us. It's not the same.' I faltered, remembering Mary's unease as we said goodbye on the first day of term. Her eagerness to be gone had been unmistakable. 'We've never called her a skivvy,' I said firmly. 'She wouldn't like it.'

'Q.E.D.' said Carpenter. 'That which had to be proved. Skivvies don't like being called skivvies.' He gave my arm a farewell squeeze. 'Don't worry about it. I won't let them hear me. I won't hurt their feelings.' He brought out the biscuits again and selected one which was almost intact. 'Go to bed,' he said. 'Dream about Doris.'

I had never heard of skivvies before I went away to boarding school. After my father died and my mother returned to teaching she still insisted on doing her own cooking, which was never ambitious (her supreme achievement was a Queen's Pudding, topped with a froth of beaten egg whites) and, to save money, she also cleaned the house, dusting the furniture every evening and basting it with lavender wax on Saturdays. Eventually my Aunt Jenny told her not to be a

fool. 'Get help,' she said and the next week Elsie Poole
arrived, interviewed and approved by my aunt, to take over
the household chores.

She was pale, thin and immaculate. Invariably, she wore
a tight black coat and a black beret with a diamanté arrow
aimed at her left eyebrow. In her shopping bag she carried
her working shoes and a flowered apron, washed and
ironed every day. Her skin was so fine that I imagined I
could see the bone beneath. She had a husband who drank
and a daughter named Little Elsie and she worked to
support them both. She scrubbed floors, polished windows
and pounded the weekly wash with a passion that was
exhilarating. Dirt was the enemy and in vanquishing it she
was scoring a victory that was moral as well as material. Her
weapons were Lifebuoy and Rinso and Reckitt's Blue. Her
saucepans, like my Aunt Ada's, were wrapped in newspaper to protect them from the grime in the air. She believed
in the power of elbow grease. It was her gospel and her
strength. She was our cleaning lady and no one would have
dared to call her a skivvy.

I did not tell Carpenter about Elsie Poole because she
belonged to another world where the customs were different and difficult for me to explain. Nor did I tell him about
my cousin Connie, my Aunt Jenny's daughter named after
my mother, who wore skirts that ended above her knee and
had married a bricklayer named Ron Cope. She rode pillion
on Ron's motor-cyle and smoked cigarettes with cork tips. I
had once heard our neighbour, Mrs Pointon, describe her as
'fast'. Somehow, I was aware, she had stepped outside the
family circle. She was still one of us, but loyalties were
strained. When her baby was born three months after her
wedding my mother and Aunt Ada debated for a whole
afternoon whether or not to send her a christening present.
'For our Jenny's sake,' said Aunt Ada. 'For no other reason.'

All the boys talked about their families and the competition to produce better and brighter credentials was
intense. Fisher had an uncle who had been presented to the
King. A boy named Perrot had an aunt who had swum the
Channel. Minton misguidedly told us of his grandmother's
cure for rheumatism. 'She soaks her hands in the jerry,' he

said. 'She says it's better than anything she gets from the doctors.'

Carpenter considered the information with some care. 'You still have piss-pots in your house then,' he said.

'My granny does. In her bedroom.'

'Piss-pot Minton,' said Carpenter. 'That's what we should call you. Pipi for short.' The nickname stuck even after Minton became an accomplished boxer, well able to take care of himself. After a while we forgot how it originated except on one Sunday when Minton's family attended evensong in the school chapel.

Carpenter studied the pews and saw an elderly lady in a sealskin coat next to Minton's mother. 'That's Minton's granny,' he decided. After the service he asked to be introduced and squeezed her hand very gently as if it were a specimen, fresh from the formaldehyde, which he was passing round in a biology class. 'She kept her gloves on,' he complained to Minton when we were back in the dormitory.

'She didn't want to be contaminated,' said Minton. It was the last word on the subject.

Carpenter himself came from the Lake District. His father, he told us, had been a doctor whose hobby had been rock-climbing. Carpenter had gone with him many times. 'It's not risky if you take care,' he said. 'You just have to know what you're doing.' He explained the various techniques, the use of ropes and crampons. 'Sometimes you're on your own, though,' he said. 'The man comes before the equipment. That's what my father used to say.'

It was a wet Saturday afternoon. Football had been rained off soon after it began and there were three hours to kill before the evening film show. The main feature was *Boys Will Be Boys* with Will Hay, prefaced by a short film about sheep farming from the Empire Marketing Board. We were in a state of high anticipation as if a party was in the offing and, like guests who had arrived too early, we cast around for something to do. The ablutions were crowded with muddy players awaiting their turn in the bath whose water was already the consistency of a thin gruel and it was impossible to reach the sanctuary of the boiler cage without making the hiding place public. The library was also full. All the draughts boards were taken and on the periodicals bench there was a queue of readers lining up for *Modern World* and *Boys' Own Paper*. We trailed through the quadrangle and into the Blacking Shed. It was the official place for cleaning shoes. One side was open to the playground. The other three walls were honeycombed with shelves and partitions containing brushes and tins of polish. Brushes were used indiscriminately, both for putting on and removing the polish and to ensure a clean head of bristles we would scrub the brush against the wall, adding to the gloss of eighty years. For as high as we could reach the walls shone like enamel. The Shed was a favourite assembly point, but not on a wet Saturday. We stood and watched the rain steam off the playground. 'Let's try the dorm,' said Carpenter. 'I'll show you what I mean about climbing.'

In the smallest dormitory, adjacent to the back stairs, there was a chimney breast which rose to the ceiling about eighteen inches away from the dividing wall. Set in the ceiling between the wall and the chimney breast was a trap door which gave access to the loft above the dormitories. 'That's where we're going,' said Carpenter, 'all the way up.'

'How high is it?' asked Fisher.

Carpenter tilted back his head. 'Thirty feet or so.'

'Where's the ladder?' I enquired.

'We don't need one,' said Carpenter taking off his blazer. 'What we do is chimney.' He braced his shoulders against the chimney breast and his feet against the opposite wall. 'All you do is walk,' he said. 'Keep yourself wedged firmly and you won't fall. One foot after the other. Like this.' He pressed backwards with his shoulders and slid six inches up the wall. His feet followed; first the left foot, then the right, leaving smears on the yellow paint like skid marks. 'And again,' he said, rising another six inches. His feet seemed to adhere to the wall as if there were suction pads on the soles of his shoes. 'It's easy,' he said, 'there's nothing to be scared of.' It was like watching a bath being filled from a hidden inlet. The level kept rising. Soon, Carpenter was above our heads. From beneath him I saw his shirt working loose from his trousers. Rain thrashed the windows and a gust of wind sobbed through the dormitory, jogging the light shades.

Carpenter squinted down at us and waved. 'Second floor, going up,' he called. The higher he climbed, the smoother his progress became. In the grey afternoon light he seemed to float the last few feet and when he knocked on the trap door, signalling that he had reached the top of the chimney the sound came as a surprise, each rap of his knuckles falling like ballast from a balloon. As we watched he slid the door to one side and heaved himself over the sill. His face appeared in the dark aperture and we saw him beckoning. 'Who's next?' he called.

No one answered. The scuff marks made by Carpenter's feet were plain on the wall, but what we had witnessed seemed impossible to imitate. Thin air lay between the floor and the ceiling. The light was fading and the wind had risen. We could hear it beyond Carpenter, blowing distantly through the ribs of the roof. A cold draught leaked down the chimney. 'Come on,' he called impatiently. 'Are you all funks?'

'You've had practice,' said Fisher. 'We've never tried.'

'Try now. You saw me do it.'

'It's too dark,' said Minton.

Carpenter's pale face bobbed towards us through the gloom.

'Do you want me to tell everyone you were scared?'

Minton sighed and peeled off his blazer. 'If I fall it's your fault,' he said. He fitted himself in the chimney as Carpenter had done and edged tentatively up the wall.

'You see,' said Carpenter, 'it's easy.'

Minton did not reply. His breathing was laboured and the pauses between each step he took grew longer. I saw his leg muscles tremble as if someone was shaking them from within. Half-way up the chimney he stopped, his hands clamped to his thighs. 'I'm stuck,' he whispered, 'I can't move.' I could hardly hear him. It seemed as though he was addressing himself, afraid that his normal tone of voice would dislodge him from where he was wedged.

'What's wrong?' demanded Carpenter.

'Minton's stuck,' I said.

Carpenter leaned through the trap door, a streak of dust branding his forehead. 'Minton,' he said softly, 'listen to me. Just do as I tell you. You'll be all right, I promise.'

Minton emitted a tiny squeak as if a bubble of air had been squeezed from his chest. His entire body shook and I realised that he was crying without making a sound.

'Start going down,' ordered Carpenter. 'Right foot first, then the left. Slowly. Keep pressing against the wall. Now your shoulders. Don't hurry. It doesn't matter how long you take. Press hard. Look straight ahead. Go a bit at a time. That's it. You're doing fine.'

Inch by inch Minton crept towards us, his feet shuddering against the gloss paint, his shirt buckling in folds up his back. Carpenter's instructions became a chant, a simple rhythm which Minton had only to follow to be saved. 'Right foot, left foot,' intoned Carpenter. 'Press hard. Don't stop.' Grudgingly, Minton descended like the last blob of sauce in a bottle. Just above our outstretched arms he fell free and as we caught him we all tumbled in a heap. My head banged against the wall. I bit my tongue. Minton's feet were astride my shoulders like the shafts of a cart. I found myself giggling. So was Fisher. So was Minton.

'Is he all right?' called Carpenter.

'All right,' I said.

We sat on the floor and watched Carpenter lower himself from the roof, adjust the trap door and skid down the chimney as smoothly as if he was sliding down one of the climbing ropes in the gymnasium. He brushed the hair from his eyes and tucked in his shirt. 'I'm glad you think it's funny,' he said.

'It's not funny,' panted Minton. 'I can't help it.' He held out his right hand and we saw his fingers quivering. 'I'm like that all over. I mean all through. I feel like a jelly.' He drew a deep, shuddering breath; then another. 'Thanks for getting me down,' he said.

Carpenter put on his blazer and shrugged it into shape. 'That's all right. It happened to me once.'

'When was that?' I asked.

Carpenter spat on his handkerchief and rubbed the smudge from his forehead. 'When I was with my father. Ages ago. It's nothing to worry about. You get over it. That's what my father said.'

The tea bell rang below us and we clattered down the stairs and into the dining hall. Mr Sleath passed us in the corridor pushing a trolley piled with cans of film. The sight of them recharged our excitement. 'Look,' said Fisher, pushing his spectacles to the end of his nose, 'Will Hay.'

Minton puffed out his cheeks and jammed his belly against the table. 'Graham Moffat,' he said.

Carpenter rolled a pellet of bread between his fingers until it was soft, then stuck it under his top lip like a solitary fang. 'Moore Marriott,' he mumbled.

I thought of his face framed by the dark rectangle of the trap door and his voice patiently spelling out the directions that had coaxed Minton down to safety. He was wrong about skivvies, I thought, but it was not important. Next term when I had eggs for tea my friend Carpenter would have the tops.

Seven

THREE WEEKS LATER we broke up for the Easter holidays. Our cases were taken to the station in the school van and we followed on the tram, in parties of fifteen or twenty with one of the masters riding herd. We had already been issued with our railway tickets and told the times of our respective trains and all that remained for us to do was find the proper platform and claim a seat. I had written to my mother insisting that no one need meet me at Stoke station but as the journey began I wondered whether I had made a mistake. In and around Wolverhampton our school uniform was a familiar sight. The stare was one of acknowledgement, not surprise. But on the train it was entirely different.

A lady sitting opposite leaned forward and, without asking if I minded, took one of my cloak buttons between her gloved finger and thumb and read the inscription aloud. She sat back and smiled. 'It's a lovely coat,' she said, 'but it must be awkward when you're playing football.' ·

I lifted my chin as the cravat bit into my throat. 'It's a cloak,' I said, 'and we don't wear it all the time. Only outside the school.'

'It's distinctive,' said the man sitting beside her. 'That's what I like about it.' He lit his pipe and through the layers of smoke that soon filled the carriage, studied me section by section.

I went into the corridor and stuck my head out of the window. Telegraph poles thudded by, streams flashed, cows raised their white faces. The station names became familiar. I saw the first pot-bank and inhaled the smell of burnt brick. When I blew my nose there was a patch of black on my handkerchief and I knew that I was nearly home.

At Stoke station I waited for the bus to take me to Burslem. In the queue behind me stood two women clutching heavy shopping baskets. One of them tapped me on the shoulder. 'Would you like a toffee?' she enquired.

I felt like a wild animal that she was trying to draw close enough to stroke. 'No thank you,' I said.

She shook the bag under my nose. 'They're butter mints. Don't you like them?'

'Yes, I do,' I said, 'but I'll be having lunch soon.'

She raised her eyebrows so that they disappeared beneath the brim of her hat. 'Lunch,' she said, 'how about that.'

Her companion shifted her basket from one hand to the other. 'That's what they call it in those posh schools,' she said. She breathed peppermint in my face. 'You mean dinner.'

'That's right,' I said, 'dinner.'

They both sucked their toffees loudly and, like the man in the train, inspected me from head to toe. Two men from a factory across the road joined the queue. 'It's a wench,' said one of them.

'Nay it's not,' said the other. 'It's a lad in a frock.'

At Burslem I changed buses and caught the single-decker that took me up the hill to Smallthorne. I walked along High Lane, my suit-case dragging my arm from its socket, and turned into our avenue. I had picked the wrong moment. Emerging from his front gate was Jim Mason, a contemporary of my father, whose claim to fame both locally and in football circles was that he had once refereed at Wembley. He had retired from the Council offices the previous year and time had begun to weigh heavily. Each day he dressed himself in his dark suit, with a stiff collar, a black silk spotted tie and a bowler hat and took up his position on the corner of the avenue. He was a tall, angular man with a wattled yellow neck and eyes puttied over with cataracts. He disliked having to wear glasses and to see who was approaching he would half-stoop and weave his head backwards and forwards like a snake preparing to strike. No one managed to pass Jim Mason without exchanging at least five minutes of small talk which could extend, unless an excuse was hastily manufactured, into half an hour. He was impervious to heat and cold. When it rained he stood guard in a long rubberized mackintosh. When slush covered the avenue in a grey pulp he wore galoshes. One summer we had a heat-wave and he exchanged his bowler hat for a straw boater. Women shoppers developed the habit of peering through their front windows before venturing out. If Mr Mason was already at his post they went down the avenue and up the next. Whenever possible I adopted the same tactic, but as I turned the corner with my suit-case I knew that there was no escape.

'Good morning Mr Mason,' I said, 'my mother's expecting me.'

He stooped and straightened, then stooped again to make sure that he knew who I was. 'My word,' he said, 'look who's here!' He tapped my cravat with his horny finger-nail and chuckled moistly, far back in his throat. 'My word,' he repeated. 'They've got you up like a dog's dinner.'

I felt myself blush. 'Everyone wears it,' I said. 'It's the school uniform.'

'I thought it might be,' said Mr Mason. He put his hands in his trouser pockets and scratched himself, first on one side then the other.

I tried not to look. 'We broke up today,' I said. 'For the holidays. I came from Wolverhampton by myself.'

'From Wolverhampton,' he said. 'It's a good service, that: I know it well. I used to referee at Molyneaux.' He stared into the middle distance for several seconds, seeing pictures which were invisible to me. 'A beautiful ground,' he said at last. 'A really nice bit of turf. It had a spring to it. Easy on the legs.' He brought me into focus again. 'Do you ever get down there? Do you see any of the matches?'

'We have our own matches,' I said. 'We have to go and cheer.'

He nodded sagely. 'Of course you do. That's to be ex-pected.' A tear rolled out of his right eye and he dabbed it with his handkerchief. He was not crying, I realised. His eyes were always watering. When there was an east wind they overflowed like the horse trough near the Wesleyan chapel.

I glanced down the avenue and saw Mary leaning over the front gate. She waved to me and, with a surge of relief, I waved back. 'I have to go,' I said. 'I'm wanted.'

Mr Mason shook my hand with great deliberation. 'If you go to Molyneaux, just mention my name. They'll remember me there.' He nodded to himself as if to confirm the memory, then tipped his hat in the direction of our house. 'Remember me to your mother,' he said.

Mary came to meet me, an apron round her waist, her stockings concertinaed around her ankles. She took hold of my case. 'Thank heavens you're here. Your mother's been watching the clock since breakfast.'

'I got stopped,' I said.

'So I noticed,' said Mary. 'That man's a blooming nuisance.' She offered her cheek. 'Give us a kiss, now you're here.'

My mother was standing at the front door, her arms open wide. She hugged me, burying my nose in the sweet-scented wool of her jumper, then held me at arm's length. 'Let me look at you.' She stroked my cloak with the flat of her hand, brushing away a scrap of lint and plucking at my belt buckle as if it was a piece of harness that needed tightening. 'It's grand,' she said, 'really grand.'

I thought of the woman on the train and the man at the bus stop and ripped the cravat from my neck. 'I hate it,' I said.

'But it's lovely.'

'It's horrible,' I shouted. 'People laugh at me.'

My mother looked up and down the avenue and closed the door before anyone heard my outburst. 'You're being silly,' she said. 'You're being as silly as they are. If people laugh it shows their ignorance. They don't know any better.'

I was spoiling it for her, I realised and I was ashamed. 'I can't tell them that,' I said more reasonably. 'They're grown-ups.'

'You must ignore them,' said my mother. 'People like that are to be pitied. You just set an example.'

It was an argument I had heard many times before. It was her comment on miners who spent their money on beer, on boys who shouted rude words in the street. She had said much the same thing one day when we had seen a man urinating in an alley beside the Coliseum Cinema in

Burslem. When I had stopped to stare she had grabbed my hand and marched on, staring straight ahead.

'It isn't fair,' I said. She made an effort and smiled. 'Don't let's worry about it now. We've got your favourite. Steak and kidney and mashed potatoes. Are you hungry?'

I seized the olive branch. 'Starving,' I said.

The house seemed to have shrunk. The walls and the ceilings boxed me in and I moved cautiously, afraid that I would knock over ornaments or collide with furniture which crowded every room. Chairs were amazingly soft. My home clothes, when I put them on, were weightless as if I was wearing gossamer. I held my tea-cup to the light and marvelled at the transparency of the china. Everything was smaller, lighter, finer than I remembered it.

'Robbie Cook asked when you were coming home,' said my mother. 'They break up next week.'

'We go back sooner,' I said, determined to nip in the bud the implication that I was better off than anyone who did not have to wear a uniform like mine.

'He wants to go to the technical school,' said Mary. 'His mother said Mr Cook was writing to the headmaster.'

I was mildly interested, but it was three months since I had seen my friends from the avenue. The time I had been away lay between us like a pool whose depth I could only guess and I hesitated before diving in. 'Robbie was always good at sums,' I said.

'And what about you?' asked my mother. 'Are you any better than you were?'

I shook my head. Mathematics bewildered me. I was literally unable to read, let alone understand, a page of figures. Orderly columns of digits and symbols filled me first with apprehension, then with blind terror. So far, the degree of my stupidity had gone unremarked, principally because Mr Smith was our maths teacher. I cribbed without being caught. The answers to the problems he set us were in the back of a text book he kept in his desk which was always unlocked. There had been no end-of-term examinations and the remarks on my progress report were so non-committal that even I found it difficult to tell whether I was being praised or blamed for my work. When the reckoning came, as I knew it would, I was confident that I would do well in the subjects I enjoyed. But I had no hope of ever comprehending mathematics. I could only hope for a miracle.

I gave my mother the report in its sealed envelope and watched her face as she read it. I was much younger than the rest of the form, a fact which Mr Gibbs had underlined in red ink, so that I had a built-in excuse for any lack of enthusiasm. But my mother was delighted. She tried to decipher the signatures and initials of the several teachers who had signed the report. 'What's he like?' she asked. 'He sounds very nice. And what about him? A bit brisk, is he?' Her interest was partly professional, one teacher assessing the style of another. But it was the document itself, spattered with percentages and peppered with opinions, which pleased her most. It was conclusive proof that I was a pupil at the school. Her fingers traced the school crest embossed on the paper. She read the motto aloud and smiled proudly when I told her what it meant. 'Without the help of the Lord we build in vain,' she repeated. 'You should remember that.' She tucked the report behind the vase in the centre of the mantelpiece beside the latest letter from Uncle Joe in America, and reached for her purse. 'Here's your pocket money,' she said and gave me a five-shilling piece. It was a thick, milled coin with a representation of Saint George killing the dragon on the picture side. I had never been given so much before. 'You deserve it,' she said, 'but make it last.'

I went to the shops that afternoon and bought a selection of the comics I was not allowed to read at school. Lionheart Logan of the Royal Mounties was still chasing villains through Canadian snow-storms in *The Wizard*. The Wolf of Kabul and his servant Chung were still decimating Pathan tribesmen in *The Hotspur*. In *The Magnet*, Tom Redwing the scholarship boy was making his mark at Greyfriars School. It was reassuring to be reminded that the world I knew had not disappeared while I had been away.

In the evening my mother sent me to Smallthorne to buy oatcakes. They were not biscuits, as I had vainly tried to explain to boys at school when we were discussing our favourite foods, but soft oatmeal pancakes, delicious with butter and honey, delectable with bacon and eggs. Chain bakeries in the Potteries made their own pale imitations, but they were too small, too skimpy to adequately enfold grease or gravy and the secret was to buy them fresh so that, wrapped in a damp tea-cloth and stored on the coldest shelf of the larder, they would last for at least three days.

The oatcake shop stood half-way down the hill, not far from the knacker's yard where we sometimes went ratting. The bottom of its bow window was level with my eyes and I would stand there for an hour at a time watching the oatcakes being made. On the far side of the shop the oatcake man measured oatmeal, flour and milk and water into tall white jugs. He added sugar and salt and yeast and when the mixture had risen he would cross over to his bakestone, a black iron plate which sent waves of heat shimmering to the ceiling, and pour out twelve liquid pats which spread and sizzled on the metal. Bubbles bulged and burst. The mouth-watering smell of toasted oatmeal seeped under the shop door and as the edges turned crisp and golden he would flip them over to cook the other side. When they were done he would stack them in a tender, tottering pile beside the bakestone and start on the next batch. As always, I bought twelve. The oatcake man wrapped them in tissue paper and I bore them home, clasped to my chest like a hot and fragrant poultice.

'Make the most of them,' said Mary when we had some for breakfast the next day, 'they'll be the last for a while.' Oatcakes were a winter food. My mother believed that they heated the blood and after March had blown itself out we bought no more until the autumn. We were only a week away from April but the weather remained cold. Snow had turned the lawn sallow and the avenue was rockier than ever, as though a glacier had ground its way from top to bottom, digging gullies in the grit, leaving behind it damson-coloured chunks of clinker and twists of pottery like cheese sticks.

'It's just as well we've not got a car,' said my mother. 'I'd be frightened to drive it down here. I told Mr Aarons to leave his at the top. He's better off walking.'

My ears pricked up. 'Who's Mr Aarons?'

'He's the optician,' said my mother. 'He's got a shop at Hanley but he's just moved next door to your Aunt Jenny. She told him I couldn't get about so he said he'd come round. I need new glasses. I'm blind as a bat.'

'Is he foreign?' I asked, already sure of the answer.

'Jewish,' said my mother. 'There are lots of Jewish opticians. They're very good at it. All he'll do here is test my eyes, but he's got his own workshop. They say he's highly skilled.'

'What sort of car has he got?'

'How should I know,' said my mother. 'It's big and it's got red leather seats.'

Not many people we knew owned cars. There were photographs of my mother and father standing beside a black Ford on the moors at Congleton. It had belonged to my father's firm and before I was born he had used it to make his rounds. When his trips became more extended and he was away for days at a time he had preferred to travel by train. Driving, he said, was too exhausting. I did not understand what he meant. Driving, as I saw it, entailed no more than sitting in comfort and turning a steering wheel. I had never ridden in the firm's car, but I still mourned its loss. 'When's Mr Aarons coming?' I asked.

'This afternoon some time. Why are you so nosey?'

'I'm not nosey,' I said. 'I've never seen anyone's eyes tested. I want to see what he does.'

Robbie Cook called for me during the morning but I was reluctant to go out in case Mr Aarons called. 'Have you seen him?' I asked Robbie. 'What does he look like?'

'I've never noticed,' he said. 'Nothing special.'

He asked to see my uniform and I took him upstairs and opened the wardrobe where it hung between my mother's dresses. 'Go on,' he said, 'put it on.'

'You can see what it's like.'

'Not properly.' He stroked the material as my mother had done. 'It's like what they wear in the Foreign Legion.'

'How d'you mean?'

'The buttons and things,' said Robbie. 'You need the cap, mind.'

'The kepi.'

'The kepi,' he agreed. We had both read *Beau Geste* and the previous summer we had all been legionnaires sniping Touaregs from behind the hillocks on the waste patch. 'What's the thing you have in your collar?' he asked.

'It's called a cravat,' I said. 'It sticks in your neck.'

'You could leave it off,' said Robbie. 'For the game, I mean.'

I studied the uniform with new interest. 'We'd need to tuck back the sides.'

'Safety pins,' he said promptly.

'And legionnaires wear long boots.'

'Wellingtons.'

In my imagination my uniform was already transformed. 'We'll try it,' I said. 'Not this afternoon. Not tomorrow, it's Sunday. Next week when you break up.'

He was looking dreamily out of the window towards a desert landscape where bullets hummed between the dunes. 'I don't know what to do about the kepi. I'll have to think.'

'And long trousers,' I said. 'We need them too.'

'That's easy.' He looked at his watch, an Ingersoll, which his parents had given him for Christmas. 'I'd best be off. I'm working at Jolley's on Saturday mornings.'

'Pinching fags in the backroom.'

'There's a packet falls off the shelf now and then.'

'And you pick it up.'

'Waste not, want not,' said Robbie. He followed me downstairs and wound his red and blue striped scarf around his neck. His mother was a champion knitter who had once won a competition in a woman's magazine. Robbie, his father and his sister Ethel had more gloves and scarves than anyone else in the avenue. Mrs Cook had tried to extend her range by making them mittens, but they had been unanimously rejected. Nobody in our avenue wore mittens.

'How about this afternoon?' said Robbie. 'We thought of going down to the cemetery to see if there were any nests.'

Burslem Cemetery, where my father lay buried, was a jungle of holly and rhododendrons where thrushes and blackbirds reared their young, foraging through beds of granite chips and jaunting over marble headstones. I had been a keen egg-collector until the previous year when I had taken home a song-thrush's egg to show to my mother. Her dismay had been unstinted. 'That poor bird,' she said. 'Imagine how she feels. Think how sad she must be.' I offered to take the egg back but my thumb pierced the shell and as I stared at the jigsaw of blue and black fragments glued to my hand I felt like a murderer. That evening my mother stared out into the garden where dusk deepened the colour of the soil and new buds gleamed through the early twilight. 'Listen to that thrush,' she said. 'It's telling you that you've killed her baby.' The bird song sobbed through the spring evening and I heard the message exactly as my mother transcribed it. 'You must never do it again,' she said. 'Never, never.'

'It's too early for nests,' I told Robbie. 'Next month maybe.'

He went to his job at Mr Jolley's and I went to the front room from where I could watch for Mr Aarons' arrival. There were other watchers in the houses opposite. Mrs Royals kept observation from her spare bedroom. Occasionally the curtains would twitch and Mrs Royals' nose would edge into view as she followed the progress of the postman from house to house. Her neighbour Mrs Sproston kept watch through her front door, held slightly ajar, while Mrs Pointon monitored the comings and goings through the leaded lights of her lounge. My mother did not share in the universal curiosity, but she received a continuous briefing from Mary, especially at night when she would interrupt her bedtime preparations to report on whose lights were still on, whether or not the car which had stopped outside Mrs Whalley's house was still there or if the gas lamp outside our front gate still had its mantle intact. Sometimes gangs of young men from Smallthorne roared down the avenue on their way home, hurling stones at the lamp as they passed. When she heard them coming Mary would rap at her window, shooing them off. It was the extent of her protest. She never dared to leave the house. After dark the avenue became no-man's land, hazardous for householders and civilians. One night two of the youths climbed the lamp post and swung from the twin arms that branched from the top, hooting like apes and drumming on their chests, their faces turned cinnamon by the gas light. Mary hammered on her window. 'Get off home,' she shouted. 'I know your fathers. I'll be round there tomorrow.' They dropped to earth, still hooting, and capered away into the darkness. Mary watched them go and padded heavily across the landing to my mother's door. 'We should tell the bobby,' she said. 'Those lads have no respect.' It was her recurrent complaint; the boys from Smallthorne cared nothing for property or persons who were outside the tribe. Mary came from the same streets; it was true that she knew their fathers. But she had renounced her kinship. Her loyalty now belonged to us and to the avenue, but there were times when her old allegiances troubled her.

As I stood staring through the lace curtains a car drew up outside the house and a man got out. He was small and slight with a pale, anxious face and a smudge of a moustache. He wore a fawn overcoat, belted at the waist, and a brown trilby hat. As he locked the car door he rested an attaché case on the bonnet and tucked a sheaf of cards, each one the size of a newspaper, under one arm. He stepped carefully over a stream of muddy water that swilled past the gate and trotted up the steps. I opened the door before he rang the bell. 'You must be Philip,' he said. 'Your mother's told me about you. She was looking forward to having you home.' He took off his hat and inserted the upper part of his body into the hall. 'She's expecting me,' he said. 'I'm Mr Aarons.'

I stepped back and he followed me, scrubbing his shoes on the mat. 'That avenue,' he said, shaking his head. 'They ought to do something about it.' He stooped to flick off a speck of mud that the mat had failed to remove. 'For this we pay rates,' said Mr Aarons.

I showed him into the dining room where my mother lay on the couch by the window. He crossed the floor before she could move. 'Don't get up. Stay right where you are. There's no need for you to move a muscle.' He took my mother's hand as if he intended to kiss it. 'And how are we today?' he asked. 'You miss nothing by being at home, believe me. Such weather!' He sighed as though some official oversight was responsible for the rain which specked the window. 'And the headaches?' he enquired. 'Are they any better?'

As my mother told him he stood by the couch, still clasping her hand, nodding sympathetically as the bulletin proceeded from eye-strain to insomnia, squeezing her fingers as if he was milking them to extract the last, unhappy drop of information. 'I see, I see,' he murmured. 'The headache comes with any reading whatever. That's dreadful. We can't allow that.' He took a torch from his pocket and shone it into her eyes, peering closely as the pupils contracted, humming to himself as he lifted the lids, then rocking back on his heels which had printed muddy crescents on the carpet.

He took a lens like a small telescope from his attaché case and studied each eye again. 'Your last prescription was how long ago?' he enquired. 'Three years? As long as that. I understand the problem. Your sister told me how difficult it was for you to get about. It must be very trying.' He set up his test cards on the sideboard and asked my mother to read the letters aloud. Silently, I read them too. He saw my lips moving and smiled.

'I can read them all,' I said, 'even the bottom line.'

'Young eyes,' said Mr Aarons as if he was giving thanks. He looked at my mother's old spectacles and clicked his tongue. 'We need to change these. They're too heavy. What you need is something lighter, more elegant.' His fingers sketched lines in the air. 'I could bring you a selection. Tortoiseshell, if you like. Gold perhaps. Whatever you decide.' He folded the glasses back into their case and snapped the lid shut. 'I'll tell you what. I'll drive you to my shop. It's no trouble. One day next week. We can do the job properly then.' He raised his hand, silencing my mother as she tried to protest. 'Not a word, no arguments. When would it be convenient?' He plucked a diary from his inside pocket and leafed through the pages. 'How about Tuesday morning? All right? Fine. Shall we say nine-thirty?' He stabbed at the page with a gold propelling pencil and nodded briskly. 'I'll be here. On the dot.'

'It's very kind of you,' said my mother. 'I don't like to be a nuisance.'

Mr Aarons frowned. 'Nuisance? Whoever mentioned being a nuisance? Believe me, it's a pleasure.' He gathered his belongings and, for the first time, noticed the marks his heels had made on the carpet. His hand flew to his mouth stifling a squeak of genuine distress. 'Your carpet,' he cried. 'See what I've done.' He dropped to his knees and scrubbed at the dirt with his finger-tips, retrieving small pellets of mud and flicking them into the fire. 'I'm sorry,' he said. 'I apologise. But that avenue!' He sighed. 'You should protest. The council should do something.'

'They've promised,' said my mother.

'Promises!' said Mr Aarons. 'They always promise!' He shuffled backwards on his knees, inspecting the pile, making sure that no mud remained. He pounced on a final crumb of dirt and stood up, satisfied. 'All gone. Now, if you have a stiff brush . . .'

'Mary will see to that,' said my mother. 'You really mustn't worry about it.'

Mr Aarons still studied the carpet and its pattern of interlocking crescents like red and blue bananas. 'Unusual,' he said.

'Hard wearing,' said my mother.

Mr Aarons stroked his moustache which was the colour of weak tea. 'These days that's important. Take children's shoes. They don't last a minute.'

'Shocking,' said my mother.

'We bought a pair for Lennie, he's five, and he was through the toes in a fortnight.'

'Children,' said my mother.

'Not children,' said Mr Aarons reproachfully. 'It was the shoes. I took them back to the shop. I complained. I wrote to the manufacturers and demanded my money back.'

'Did you get it?'

'Certainly I got it.' He tapped his attaché case. 'This very morning. Full reimbursement *and* a letter of apology.'

I could tell that my mother was impressed. Rising prices

and shoddy goods were constant themes in her conversations with my aunts. A man who not only shared her resentment, but went on to demand and receive satisfaction was to be admired. 'It's the only thing to do,' she said. 'We take too much lying down.'

Mr Aarons tightened the belt of his overcoat. It had no buttons, I realised. The garment was swagged together like a dressing gown. 'You should let them know about your avenue,' he said. 'That's why we pay rates. They're taking money under false pretences.'

'We've tried,' said my mother. 'I know Mr Mason's had a word with the council. He's told them. He knows the right people.'

I saw Mr Aarons' face freeze into a mask of total disbelief. 'The right people are the ones who get things done. Mr Mason has been talking to the wrong people.'

'He was on the council,' said my mother. 'He was on it for years.'

Mr Aarons' smile was like a ripple on the surface of a lake, signalling underwater tremors too deep to interpret. 'Naturally,' he said. He picked up his case and tucked his cards under his arm. He bowed from the waist. 'Until next week,' he said.

I saw him to the front door and watched him daintily pick his way to his car. He took a rag from the dashboard and wiped his shoes before taking his seat. 'The right people,' he said, shaking his head. He wound down the window and waved goodbye. I wanted to tell him that Mr Mason was standing guard at the top of the avenue and that he would be interested to hear what Mr Aarons had to say about the council, but the moment passed before I could find the words. The car bounced gently over the potholes and turned the corner. The horizon seemed to waver and bend at the edges. I looked at the avenue with new eyes. I had met my first Jew.

Eight

THE NEXT DAY I met Mrs Aarons. When I awoke the sun was buttering the walls of my bedroom and for a while I lay with the blankets up to my nose, planning what I might do. For a start, there was the Marlpit to revisit. It was half a mile away behind the Michelin garages at the far end of High Lane, a ragged hole in the ground traversed by trenches and earthworks, where mechanical diggers had scooped out the raw clay for plates and teapots. We had played there since I could remember, too far from any house to be overlooked, hidden by tall thickets of hawthorn whose branches we could tether and shroud with sacks and clods of earth to make shelters smelling of soil and hessian. We lit fires and roasted potatoes and pignuts in the embers. In the autumn we stalked each other through plantations of willow herb, marking tracks by the silvery explosions of seed which curled away on the breeze like woodsmoke. The banks of the pit were seamed with narrow bands of snail shells, pearly and iridescent, which crumbled at a touch. They shone like the lustre vases brought home by my father. It was a more exciting place to play than the waste patch because it was secret. But then I remembered; it was Sunday. Rough play was forbidden and I had to attend morning service at Hill Top.

Since my mother had given up going to chapel we no longer had a pew of our own and I sat with my Uncle Arthur, Aunt Jenny's husband, who made shorthand notes of the sermon and hummed the tunes of the hymns instead of singing the words. Rain or shine, we always walked to chapel, ostensibly for the exercise but also because my uncle held that it was wrong to ride on a bus which employed drivers and conductors who, if they obeyed the Ten Commandments, should regard the Sabbath day as holy and do no labour. We would meet at the top of the avenue and proceed down Macclesfield Street, through the park and past the recreation ground. On Sundays the swings were chained together so that no one could use them. The roundabout was padlocked, a plank was fixed to the centre of the slide and the see-saw was bolted to the ground. If we were early we would make a detour round the lake. There was an island in the middle on which a pair of swans attempted to nest every year, but without fail the eggs were stolen or smashed by stones thrown from the bank. A green-painted aviary overlooked the lake. It smelled of dusty radiators and bird droppings and comprised one long cage which contained several canaries and budgerigars, a sulphur-crested cockatoo and, for a short time, a toucan. One Sunday on our way to chapel I looked through the window and saw it lying dead on the floor. My uncle called at the park-keeper's lodge to report the casualty. 'I'm not surprised,' said the park-keeper. 'I caught some lads feeding it toffees yesterday.'

To sustain me through the sermon I was allowed not toffees but three Fox's Glacier Mints which were doled out to me by a sidesman named Mr Parr. He had a crest of white hair like a shaving brush and he wore a pink hearing aid in one ear. 'Don't crunch those mints,' he told me, 'make them last.' It was good advice. With careful husbanding I could hoard a tiny transparent wafer under my tongue until I knew for certain that the sermon was drawing to a close. Then, as the minister said 'Amen', I would bite down on the last of the mint, celebrating my imminent release as I reached for Hymns Ancient & Modern.

We walked back through the town. The public houses would be sweeping out, readying themselves for opening time and it was as though in some back street a giant was heaving himself awake, yawning prodigiously and sending his stale breath gusting from every saloon bar and snug. For my uncle, who was an ardent teetotaller, it was a testing experience. Outside the Stafford Arms oysters of phlegm studded the pavement. Passing The Leopard we skirted tawny piles of broken glass where bottles had been shattered in arguments the night before. By the time we reached Burslem railway station the air was clearer and as we climbed the hill to Smallthorne I would see my uncle opening his nostrils like a horse scenting home pastures.

He was an uncommonly reserved man with a port-wine complexion and a beard so dark that, even shortly after shaving, the stubble on his cheeks looked like powder burns. His eyes were large and heavily lidded and at family gatherings, in which he took little part, I would often see him sitting to one side, a cup of tea lodged in his lap, apparently dozing. He gave the impression of conserving speech and movement as if he had taken a vow never to waste breath or energy.

People meeting him for the first time wondered how he had come to marry my Aunt Jenny. She was my mother's favourite sister, gossipy and extravagant, an impulsive giver of presents, with a neat monkey face and a fondness for bright, filmy dresses and delicate shoes. 'He got her on the rebound,' Mary told me once when I went on and on about how different they were.

'The rebound from what?'

'Never you mind,' she said. 'See if anyone wants more tea.'

Eventually I understood what she meant and it helped to explain Uncle Arthur's look of melancholy. I felt he was sad that he had not been my aunt's first choice, besides which, said my mother, he had never completely got over the loss of their eldest daughter, Margaret, who had died when she was fourteen. Margaret's sayings were often repeated when family anecdotes were told; how, for example, she had seen a herd of cows caked with their own dung and asked why no one wiped their bottoms. Margaret was the brilliant, the beautiful one and when her memory was invoked it was always with a note almost of surprise that she was the child of such a dull dog as my uncle.

I certainly found him dull, but restful too. He never criticized me. On our walks to and from Hill Top he let me chatter without once interrupting. Our silences were companionable. I never felt I had to make conversation or try to impress him. No one, it seemed, thought he was worth impressing, although he was rich, a director of one of the biggest of the local pottery firms with a head for figures that I found awesome. My mother once suggested that he should help me with my sums, but he refused. 'You're the teacher, Connie,' he said. 'I don't have the knack of passing it on.'

His eyes swivelled in my direction like tortoises squinting out of their shells and, without warning, he winked. It was done too deliberately for me to suppose I had imagined it. But he said no more until our next walk to the chapel. Then, as we set off, our heads bowed against the wind that tore down the avenue he jogged my elbow. 'You're not to worry about sums,' he said.

'But I can't do them.'

'Some people can't. It's not in their nature.'

'You can. Mother says you can do them all in your head.'

He gripped the brim of his bowler hat as we approached High Lane. The wind reached gale force there and fell as soon as we crossed the road. 'I never had to learn,' he said. 'It came naturally, but I can't show anyone else.' He settled his hat more comfortably on his head. 'Anyhow,' he said, 'I didn't think you'd want to be bothered. 'There's enough folk who want to teach you things.'

My uncle was not the best person to ask about the Aarons. Although they were his neighbours he was too shy to have introduced himself and too polite to tell me of any excitement their arrival may have occasioned. My Aunt Jenny was less reticent. After the service I called to see her before going home. She mixed me a glass of Eiffel Tower lemonade, adding sugar and cold water and stirring the mixture with a silver spoon. The yellow crystals dissolved slowly, streaking the water like oil and she held it against the light before giving it to me to taste. 'See if it's sweet enough,' she said.

I took a tentative sip. 'Not quite.'

She added more sugar. 'You'll rot your teeth,' she warned. 'Your mother'll be after me.'

'Never,' I said fondly.

She leaned against the kitchen mangle, watching me drink. The mangle was made of cast iron with massive wooden rollers which I was always being warned not to touch. Mrs Davenport, who did my aunt's washing, had once trapped her finger between them squashing it flat and the same thing would happen to me, I was told, if I did not leave well alone. 'You've seen him then,' said my aunt.

'Who d'you mean?'

'Mr Aarons. He wants you to pop in. He has a note for your mother.'

'What about?' I asked.

'How should I know,' said Aunt Jenny. 'Maybe it's a love letter.'

I snorted with laughter and the lemonade went up my nose. 'Fat chance,' I said. 'It's about her glasses.'

My aunt nodded mysteriously. 'Wait and see.'

'What are they like?' I demanded.

She nodded again, deepening the mystery. 'Different,' she said.

'How d'you mean?'

'All sorts of ways. They drink lemon tea. In a glass.' She pointed to my lemonade. 'Like that. No milk. Just tea and a slice of lemon.'

The idea sounded preposterous. 'You're having me on,' I said.

'And Mrs Aarons has three fur coats,' said my aunt.

'Three!'

'I've seen them. She asked me in and showed me.'

It was a measure of my aunt's interest in the Aarons that she had not yet asked me about school. I decided to put that right. 'Our headmaster told us about Jews,' I said. 'And our form master.'

'And what did they say?'

'That they've not got the killer instinct.'

'I should hope not,' said my aunt. 'Who on earth wants that?' She steered me into the next room. 'What else do they teach you at that school?' she asked.

For half an hour I told her. She went on preparing lunch, peeling potatoes and slicing carrots. 'You're doing all right then,' she said.

'Right enough. I got a good report.'

'I'll be along to see it. Tomorrow perhaps. Tell your mother around tea-time.' She glanced at the wall clock. 'You'd best get that note from Mr Aarons before they start eating.'

Only a privet hedge stood between my aunt's house and the Aarons and I could see her watching, standing well back in her kitchen, when I knocked on their back door. Mr Aarons let me in. 'Don't be a stranger,' he said, 'come inside.' He seemed to have shrunk slightly since the previous day until I realised that although he had shed his fawn overcoat the clothes he was now wearing – a cardigan, shirt and slacks – were all the same colour. Everything matched, but his size was reduced by one layer. 'I just wanted to let your mother know there's been a little upset on Tuesday,' he said. 'Nothing serious. An hour's difference at the most. The thing is we've got a new fridge coming and I want to be here when they deliver it.' He pointed to a sleek cream cabinet that stood against the wall crooning to itself. 'That's got to go. We brought it with us from Birmingham and it's not right for this kitchen.' He wrenched the door open and contemplated rows of milk bottles, a joint of meat, eggs in bright wire hammocks, a chocolate cake oozing cream. Everything looked cleaner, sweeter, fresher than in the pantry at home. I remembered my mother saying that no one really needed a refrigerator. It was not only a luxury but an extravagance. But I was witnessing a dream. The Aarons' refrigerator reminded me of things seen in American films; cocktail cabinets, chrome and leather stools, cars which were called roadsters, ice-cream sundaes. It was a glimpse of another world. Mr Aarons slammed the door and the refrigerator's croon became a chuckle. 'They don't service it properly,' he complained. 'For what they charge you'd think they'd do it right.'

'I suppose so,' I said.

'You don't have one, do you?' said Mr Aarons. 'Very sensible. They're more trouble than they're worth. Possessions mean headaches. Not like your mother's. Worries, rather. The more you have the more you have to take care of.' He did not sound too burdened by his responsibilities.

'Give the boy a lolly,' called a voice from another room.

Mr Aarons stood to attention. 'Give me a chance,' he said. He opened the refrigerator again and pulled down the flap of a compartment I had not previously noticed. 'What flavour?' he asked. 'We've got orange, raspberry, lime.'

'I've never tasted lime,' I said.

He gave me an icy green tablet impaled on a stick. I licked it tentatively, then bit off the first half inch. 'Don't spoil your appetite,' said Mr Aarons.

'Spoil? What's to spoil?' demanded the other voice. 'He's a growing boy. Why don't you bring him through.'

Mr Aarons steered me into the next room which, at first glance, seemed to be full of flowers. There were lilies, both orange and white, in a cut-glass vase in the centre of the table. On a radiogram in one corner there stood a bowl of roses. On the sideboard there was an arrangement of pampas grass and peacock feathers in a brass canister. By the fireplace where a basket of artificial logs glowed in the grate there was a plantation of cacti growing in a miniature desert. A lady in a black silk dress was rearranging the terrain, sprinkling sand from a trowel and planting pebbles to build tiny mountains. 'Let me look at you,' she said.

My nose was level with her stomach. When she embraced me it was like being pressed face downwards into a firm rubber mattress smelling of soap and bath salts. I could feel ribbing of some sort against my cheek and when she released me I saw the outline of laces and buttonholes beneath her dress. I looked up over a large brooch, a powdery expanse of chest and into the face of Mrs Aarons. Her nose was large, her eyes were lustrous and her hair was glossy and black. 'You didn't tell me he was such a big boy,' she exclaimed, hugging me again. I heard her stomach rumble and struggled free. 'Don't tell me you're too big for a hug,' she said.

I showed her the lolly. 'It's melting. I didn't want to get it on your dress.'

She swooped into action. 'Bring a flannel. Wipe his hands. Don't just stand there.' Her commands buffeted Mr Aarons as though he was being hit with a pillow. He dodged from side to side, then pulled a handkerchief from his pocket and wiped my fingers, one by one. 'Is he dry?' she demanded. 'We don't want to send him home sticky.'

'It's all right now,' I said.

'You're sure?'

'Quite sure.'

'Then sit down.' She lowered herself on to the settee and patted the cushion beside her. 'Tell me about yourself.'

'I've just been to chapel,' I said. 'I went with my uncle next door.'

'That's nice,' said Mrs Aarons. 'And your mother. How is she?'

It was a question I was always being asked. 'About the same, thank-you.'

Mrs Aarons sighed. 'Poor lady. You must be a good boy for her sake.'

'I know,' I said.

'Such a brave person. Your aunt tells me. And you away at school. How can she bear it?'

'She says it's a wonderful opportunity,' I said.

Mrs Aarons looked fiercely at her husband. 'Did you hear that? I ask you. What a woman to think only of her child. To want what's best for him.' She glared around the room. 'Does she like flowers?'

'Oh, yes,' I said.

'Very well then, she shall have flowers.' She plucked the lilies from their vase, ignoring the wet stems that dripped on to the table. 'And roses? Does she like them?' She emptied the bowl and thrust the blooms into a sheet of newspaper. 'Hot-house, tell her. They don't like the cold. Put an aspirin in the water. It makes them last longer.' She wrapped more paper around the bundle and laid it in my arms. 'Hurry home to your mother,' she said. 'Give her my love.' Mr Aarons opened the door to the kitchen but she pointed in the other direction: 'Let him out the front.' I stammered my thanks but the compliment, I realised, was not intended for me. It was in honour of my mother.

My aunt was watching I was certain, but I did not look back as I hurried along High Lane clutching the flowers. I sped past Mr Mason who was on the corner monitoring the traffic and reached our back door without seeing anyone else. 'Where on earth are those from?' asked my mother when I heaped the flowers on to the draining board.

'From Mrs Aarons. She sends her love.'

'Mrs Aarons! What were you doing there?'

I produced the envelope which Mr Aarons had slipped into my pocket before I left. 'Aunt Jenny said I had to collect this. She said it might be a love letter.'

My mother snatched it from my hand. 'Don't be daft.' She skimmed through the brief message and shook her head. 'It says nothing about the flowers.'

'There's pounds-worth here,' said Mary.

'Mrs Aarons told me to tell you they were hot-house,' I said. 'They don't like the cold.'

Mary raised her eyebrows. 'Tell us something new.' She counted the roses, stroking the petals with her stubby fingers. 'Would you believe it. There's a dozen.'

'It's too much,' said my mother. 'Far too much.' She gripped my shoulder and shook it quite hard. 'Did she say anything else when she gave you the flowers?'

I tried to remember the sequence. 'She was sorry you were ill. She said you were a brave person and she called you a poor lady.'

'Did she indeed.'

'She said I should be good for your sake. And Mr Aarons gave me an ice lolly.'

'I've told you about eating between meals,' said my mother.

'Mrs Aarons said it wouldn't spoil my appetite. She said I was a growing boy.'

'Fancy that,' said Mary. She took a green glass vase from the cupboard and filled it with water. 'I'll put the lilies in this, shall I?'

'I don't know that I want them,' said my mother.

Mary measured the lilies against the vase and snipped at their stems with the kitchen scissors. 'Why ever not?'

'You know why not,' said my mother.

'She means well,' said Mary.

'It's not what she means. It's what she does.' My mother brooded for a moment. 'And what she says. Have you ever heard anything like it? I'll give her poor lady!'

I was bewildered by the turn of events. I knew that my mother had a hot temper and that she was unpredictable, but I could not understand why she was so enraged by Mrs Aarons' kindness. I thought, perhaps, that I might be able to distract her. 'Mr Aarons showed me their refrigerator,' I said. 'The one they're getting rid of. It's not right for their kitchen.'

'Mr Aarons said that, did he?'

I nodded. 'They're getting a new one on Tuesday. That's why he's going to be late.'

I saw my mother's face turn bright red. The change of colour was so sudden it was as though she was playing our dormitory game of blowing on a lighted torch, turning our cheeks into lanterns. 'Some people!' she said.

Mary started on the roses, cracking their stems with the bottom of a milk bottle. 'Mrs Aarons said you were to put an aspirin in the water,' I said. 'It makes them last longer.'

Mary and my mother exchanged glances. I imagined unspoken sentences swelling between them like a hot-air balloon I had seen being inflated on a news-reel. Their disapproval seemed to fill the room. 'Does it?' I asked finally. 'Does it make them last longer?'

'Some folk say it does,' said Mary, 'but a half-penny in the water's just as good. Especially for anemones.'

'They're what I like,' said my mother. 'Anemones. Better than all your fancy flowers.' She put her arm around my waist. 'You bought some for my birthday. Do you remember that?'

'I remember.' My mother's birthday was in October. Years ago my father had given her an opal ring. It was her birth stone, she said, unlucky for anyone else to wear.

'You'll be away at school this year,' she said. 'We'll have to celebrate before you go back.'

I tried to look enthusiastic. Birthdays and Christmases spent at home were invariably tame, but they were occasions which it would have been unthinkable to ignore. To my mother they represented the family united against the world; times when slights were forgiven, bonds fortified. By invoking her birthday she was reminding us both where our pride and our loyalties lay. We were not to be flattered or bought. Intuitively we put first things first. Anemones came before lilies; hot-house flowers were for people who could pay for them. The logic was simple and harsh and comforting. She picked up the paper in which the roses had been wrapped and smoothed it flat on the kitchen table. 'It'll do for the fire,' she said.

I glanced at the photograph half-covered by her hand and saw a street in which a group of people were standing by a large shop window. I could not understand what the picture showed. Some of the people were laughing, some had their backs turned to the camera. One man held a paint brush and behind him on the shop front was inscribed a star made by daubing one triangle on top of another. My mother folded the paper into a narrow dart. Then pleated it from left to right to make a firelighter. She tossed it into the kindling box. 'The rubbish some people read,' she said.

Nine

MY MOTHER'S irritation with Mrs Aarons did not last. She did not change her mind about the virtues of living simply and her loyalty to the family remained absolute, but she had never experienced a wave of compassion so powerful as that unleashed by Mrs Aarons and she was overwhelmed. On Tuesday Mrs Aarons was waiting in the car to take my mother to the optician's. She wrapped a rug round my mother's knees and wedged a cushion behind her head. 'So you'll be comfortable,' she said. Later that morning she brought her home but she would not come inside the house. At the front door my mother waved her goodbye, then turned to face Mary and me, her face rueful, a large box of chocolates clasped in her hand.

On Wednesday a jar of calf's-foot jelly was delivered by the grocer's errand boy. On Thursday there came a bunch of freesias, sheathed in cellophane, their stalks lagged in damp cotton wool. Then on Friday Mrs Aarons herself called to deliver a small parcel of freshly-sliced ham and a sponge cake from Swinnertons. 'A little something for your tea,' she said.

My mother was, quite literally, speechless. Within the family there was a constant exchange of small gifts. Ada knitted gloves. My mother made marmalade. Jenny's lemon curd went the rounds in small dumpy jars. There was nothing unusual in giving and receiving presents. But the traffic went in all directions. It was an embarrassment to be the one who received most and gave least. It was as if they were playing Pass the Parcel. The one who was left holding it when the music stopped lost the game.

Competition was fierce, with my cousins occasionally joining in. Points were scored when my cousin Jessie, Uncle Ernest's daughter, took me on an outing to Trentham Gardens with her friend Pan or when Hilda, Aunt Ada's daughter took me to the Regent Cinema in Hanley and for coffee in the restaurant afterwards. My mother retaliated by sending off packets of embroidered handkerchiefs and lavender sachets. Hilda was presented with a Jacqmar scarf. It was important to reciprocate, to maintain a balance. The game was played according to the rules and although they were not made explicit they were scrupulously observed.

Mrs Aarons' largesse was so unexpected that my mother was caught off balance. She was like the citizen of a city under siege who was bombarded one day with bread instead of boulders. She could not throw it back; the assault was too persistent. There was no time to take shelter or consider strategy. The loaves rained down and my mother watched in amazement. Like it or not, she had a benefactor.

She asked Aunt Jenny's advice. 'I don't know the woman from Adam,' she said. 'Why is she doing all this?'

My aunt nibbled on a ratafia. Although she accused me of putting too much sugar in my lemonade she had a sweet tooth herself. 'She told me she likes to share her good fortune,' she said.

'Why with me?'

'Why not you?' She dipped the biscuit in her coffee. 'She enjoys giving things.'

'So do I when I can afford it,' snapped my mother, 'but look at it all.' She motioned towards the flowers, the calf's-foot jelly and the chocolates which she had resolutely refused to eat. 'She makes me feel like a charity case. You'll have to talk to her.'

My aunt licked the biscuit sugar from her fingers. 'What would I say?'

'Tell her I'm embarrassed. Tell her we don't do things this way.'

'She wouldn't understand that. You'd hurt her feelings.'

'What about *my* feelings?'

'She's doing no harm, Connie,' said my aunt. 'I don't suppose it will go on. You'll have to put up with it for a while.'

Sisterly feelings never constrained my aunts or my mother from letting fall the occasional tart reminder that one or the other was protesting too much and that it was time to draw the line. Since she had become an invalid my mother's complaints were taken more seriously than they might otherwise have been. But sometimes they sounded a note of petulance which stung my aunts into reasserting their authority. As girls they had washed my mother's face and brushed her hair and put her to bed. They were grown women now, marked by marriage and birth and death but the years had no relevance. My mother was still their little sister. They would love her and protect her because she was family and by the same token they would correct her when she misbehaved. They were the older girls and it was their job.

My mother's mouth set in a dangerous line. She hated being criticized or contradicted, but she saw that no support was forthcoming from my aunt. She could like it or lump it. 'It all started with you,' she said crossly. 'You sent that man here to see my eyes. I didn't ask him to interfere.'

Aunt Jenny smacked her on the knee, calling her to attention. 'He offered to come. Don't be so ungracious.'

'That woman, then. You're not saying that's the same.'

'I've told you, Connie. She believes in sharing. And she's got plenty to share.'

I thought of the Aarons' house with the refrigerator humming in the kitchen and the electric fire burning at full blast instead of the single red bar with which my mother tried to warm her bedroom. I thought of the flowers and the fur coats and the car with its leather upholstery and together they spelled a way of life so prodigal, so contrasting to ours that it seemed not only wilful of my mother to reject any part of it, but timid too. The Aarons affected me like loud music and bright colours. To ignore them was like walking away from a parade. I did not want to join it, but I wanted to watch. I was eager, not for gifts but for novelty. As my aunt said, they were different. Compared to our style of family greeting in which kisses were exchanged as briskly as sparrows pecking up crumbs, Mrs Aarons' embrace had drenched me like a strong foreign sun. The memory still lingered. I recalled the texture of her dress and beneath it her body rigged like a ship, but still plump and elastic. I did not want it all to go away.

'The other thing is, she needs friends,' said Aunt Jenny.

'She can buy all she wants,' said my mother.

Aunt Jenny took my mother's hand. 'That's not Christian.'

'Neither is she.'

'That's not worthy of you Connie,' said my Aunt.

Tears sparkled in my mother's eyes and she looked crossly out of the window. 'It's always me that's wrong.'

'This time it is.'

'I can't help what I feel.'

'Nor can she. It's up to you to understand.'

'It's easy for you,' said my mother. 'You're not stuck inside four walls all day. I have to sit here and be glad if people come to me.'

'You'd like it less if they didn't,' said Aunt Jenny.

'That's not fair.'

'Nor are you,' said my aunt. They stared hard at each other, then Aunt Jenny put her arms round my mother and pressed her face into the crook of her shoulder. She stroked the back of my mother's head. 'There, there,' she said, 'don't take on.'

I heard Mary come into the room behind me. Without a word she seized my elbow and pulled me into the kitchen. She closed the door deliberately. 'You leave them be,' she said. 'Your mother's upset. They don't want you standing there gawking.'

'I wasn't gawking.'

'Your eyes were popping out of your head,' she said. 'They'll sort it out better without you there.'

She sent me off to the shops with a list of groceries she did not need and as I left Machin's the fruiterers, where oranges were cheaper than at Mr Jolley's, I saw Robbie Cook turn the corner of Dartmouth Street. He carried a pudding basin and a bundle of newspapers under his arm and I fell in beside him as he mounted the steps of Cooper's fish and chip shop. The paintwork was dark green and the bottom halves of the windows were covered with a transfer which looked like blue and white clouds. From the pavement it was impossible to see inside the shop, but within the radius of half a mile it announced its business with the smell of frying batter which on winter days coiled through the surrounding streets like a noose drawing the customers in.

Inside the shop Mr Cooper in his shirt sleeves and braces and Mrs Cooper in a white overall like a nurse's uniform tended their cauldrons of molten fat, shovelling in pallid loads of potatoes and dredging out mountains of golden chips. Robbie pushed his bowl along the counter. 'Two portions of peas, two rock salmon, one cod, one plaice and a shilling's worth of chips,' he said.

'Please,' said Mr Cooper, who was a stickler for manners.

'Please,' said Robbie.

'And how's your mother?' Mr Cooper asked me.

'About the same as usual, thank-you,' I said. 'Do you have any frits, please.'

'We'll see,' said Mr Cooper, trailing the slices of fish through a trough of flour and plunging them into the fat. Frits were the rock hard remnants of batter left over when the frying was done. They were sold to favoured customers at a penny a bag. Sometimes, if he was impressed by a child's politeness, Mr Cooper gave them away free. We watched him parcel up the chips, swaddling them in Robbie's newspapers, and decant two ladles of peas into his bowl from a vat simmering at the end of the range. He wrapped the fish separately, took Robbie's money and assumed a look of surpassing innocence. 'Have I forgotten something?' he enquired.

'The frits,' we said in chorus.

'Ah, yes,' said Mr Cooper. 'The frits.'

He filled a paper cornet with the savoury fragments and waved away my penny. 'Don't spill them on the floor. It's just been swept,' he said.

We walked up Dartmouth Street, Robbie balancing his parcels on top of the bowl of peas, pausing occasionally while I fed him frits. At the last stop he licked his greasy lips. 'I've got an idea for the kepi,' he said. 'There's this old cap of my dad's. He had it when he worked for the gas company. It's got a proper peak and everything. All we need to do is stick a handkerchief on the back for the sun-shade.'

'Won't he mind us having it?'

'We'll only be borrowing it,' said Robbie. 'We'll give it back.'

'This afternoon then?'

'If you like. Can you get the cloak all right?'

My heart gave a lurch. I did not want to explain the Foreign Legion game to my mother. 'I'll sneak it out.'

'You're sure?'

'Of course I'm sure.' To admit any uncertainty would be to lose face.

'All right, then,' said Robbie. 'About two o'clock. I'll get the others.'

When I arrived home my aunt had left and my mother was lying on the couch with a travelling rug drawn up to her waist. 'She's taken some tablets,' said Mary. 'Just to calm her down. We'll eat here in the kitchen.'

I was not alarmed or even surprised. My mother frequently took tablets which she said were for her nerves. They were kept in a brown medicine bottle in the sideboard and Mary had warned me never to interfere with them. When I asked why not she looked solemn. 'You'd be a goner, that's why.'

'What about my mother?'

'The doctor tells her how many to take. That's what it says on the bottle. Do not exceed the stated dose. It's if you take too many you're in trouble.'

After taking the tablets my mother often dozed for an hour or so. She disliked going to bed during the day because it removed her from the normal business of the house and she was reminded even more emphatically that she was an invalid. The couch was her compromise, a place to which she could retire without making herself conspicuously absent. She lay somewhere on the edge of sleep, undisturbed by the click of crockery and the rush of taps but alert to any knock on the door and instantly suspicious if the visitor chose not to come in. 'Who is it?' she would call.

'No one,' Mary would reply.

'It can't be no one.'

'Nobody that matters.'

'I'll decide who matters.'

At which point Mary would roll her eyes and poke her head round the door to deliver a bulletin on who had called, what they had said and why it was nothing for my mother to excite herself about. 'She'll be the death of me,' she told me more than once.

Mary enjoyed eating in the kitchen because the meal, however makeshift, was her private feast. She was innocently greedy, hoarding leavings and scraps of offal which, with some ingenuity, she would transform into what she described as 'a bit of knife and fork'. Lunch might comprise a single sausage, a kidney, a fragment of liver, some bacon shavings and a tomato from which she would first remove the seeds. If she missed one it would invariably work its way beneath her plate and she would have to take out her false teeth and rinse them under the tap. The bacon was always grilled so that the fat collected in the pan as a pool of dip which she would mop up either with an oatcake or a slice of bread. She talked to herself as she prepared the meal, shushing the sausage when it spat back at the grill, begging the liver not to burn, telling the kidney not to split as it swelled beneath the flame. Sometimes she would coddle brains with butter, adding a pinch of dry mustard and spreading the mixture on toast. She was also fond of pig's trotters and tripe, dousing them with malt vinegar and dusting them heavily with pepper and salt. My mother told her she ate too much. 'It's why you're always out of puff,' she said. But Mary, who heeded my mother's advice on almost every other matter, took no notice. Eating was her purest pleasure and she would not be denied.

While my mother drowsed in the next room she made us a welsh rarebit, leaving the cheese beneath the grill until it bubbled and browned, shunting the toast on to warm plates and daubing it with picalilli before slicing off the first pungent morsel. She ate busily, chasing stray crumbs and polishing one half of the plate before moving on to the next section. 'Nice bit of cheese,' she said between mouthfuls.

'Lovely,' I agreed.

'You'll not get anything like this at your school.'

I shook my head. 'Nothing like it.'

'Mind you,' said Mary, 'with all those lads it can't be easy.' She stabbed the last square of toast and popped it into her mouth. 'Now,' she said, 'how about a nice cup of tea?'

She was scalding the pot when Robbie Cook knocked at

the back door. I looked to see if he was carrying his father's cap but he motioned with his head when Mary went into the larder to fetch the milk jug. 'I left the things outside,' he hissed. 'What about your cloak?'

'It's upstairs.'

'How are you going to get it out?'

I had already decided. 'I'll chuck it through the window. You be there to catch it.'

'I've got the pins,' he said. 'And my wellingtons. You'd best bring yours too.'

'We're going to the marlpit,' I told Mary. 'Can we have some matches?'

She plucked unhappily at her bottom lip. 'You'll get me shot. You know what your mother thinks about you lighting fires.'

'We'll take care,' said Robbie.

'Just a few,' I coaxed.

She counted out half a dozen from a box by the stove. On the cover there was a picture of a man wearing a striped bathing costume. His name was Captain Webb and my mother said he had been a champion swimmer. I often wondered why his portrait should be on a box of matches. 'And keep out of the smoke,' said Mary. 'I don't want you back here smelling like a kipper.'

We put on our jackets and went down the steps into the yard. 'Hang on,' I said loudly to Robbie, 'I've just got to get a handkerchief.' I dashed past Mary, up the stairs and into my mother's bedroom. I took the cloak from her wardrobe and opened the landing window. Robbie was in the yard below. 'Catch,' I said and dropped the cloak into his arms. We ran down the avenue and along the unmade road which ran parallel to High Lane. It was a slightly longer and more hazardous route to the marlpit, taking us through a new estate on which Freddie Steele the Stoke City footballer had just bought a house and over building plots corralled with chestnut palings and barbed wire. We knew fewer people there who would recognise us, but there was also the risk of running into the estate gang with whom we waged a vendetta whose intensity varied- with the film which was showing at the Palace that week. If it was a western with

Indians we had to keep a look out for ambushes. If it was a war film we had to expect a grenade attack with clods of earth aimed from behind the piles of bricks which traced the coming boundaries of the estate.

No one waylaid us. At the marlpit Roy Greaves and Edwin Jones were waiting. Roy had an air-rifle and Edwin a bayonet which he had tied to a broom-stick. The blade was pitted with rust which he said was the blood of Germans his uncle had killed in the war. They greeted me warily. We had not seen each other since I went away to school and we inspected each other for signs of change. 'They've given you a right crop,' said Roy finally.

'It's the school barber,' I said.

'Convict ninety-nine,' said Edwin.

Robbie unfolded the cloak and I put it on. He buttoned it to my chin and pinned back the skirt on either side so that my knees were bare. 'Now the cap,' he said. He had glued a square of muslin to the back so that it hung down over my shoulders. His father's head was bigger than mine and to prevent the cap sliding over my ears he had padded it with newspaper. I tilted it to a more rakish angle. 'How's that?' I asked.

Robbie stepped back a pace and looked me up and down. 'It'll do.'

'We'll change over later,' I said. 'Let's get the fire lit.'

Roy and Edwin had already made a small pyramid of paper and sticks within a brick surround. I struck a match and we squatted down while the flames took hold. 'You two are the Riffs,' said Robbie, 'and we're the legionnaires. You're raiding the fort and we've got to hold you off till reinforcements come.'

'When will that be?' asked Edwin.

'When you hear the bugle.' Robbie pursed his lips and sounded the call. 'Another thing,' he told Roy. 'We want no pellets in that gun. My mother says they can put your eye out.'

Roy looked sulky. 'I won't point it at you.'

'No pellets,' said Robbie. I always felt safe when he was organising a game. His imagination raced ahead of mine, but it was sensitive to hazards which would never have occurred to me. 'Go on then,' he said. 'We'll count to twenty, then you can start the raid.'

We shut our eyes as Roy and Edwin scampered away. We were in a gulley with a hump at its centre in which was buried the remains of a large iron drum, all that was left of the machinery that had been installed when the marlpit was being quarried. The walls of the drum were waist-high. There were holes where massive bolts had been gnawed loose by time and weather and, lying flat, we could use them as rifle slots through which to snipe at the enemy. The attack, we thought, was most likely to come from above. Hawthorns and willow-herb grew to the edge of the pit and it was easy to crawl to the very rim without being seen. Our fort, though, was fifty yards or more from the cliff wall and anyone charging down from the top could be picked off before reaching us. We hauled two sheets of corrugated iron over the top of the drum so that we had a roof over our heads and squinted through the bolt holes.

For several minutes nothing happened then, without warning, a volley of clods rained down from the shelter of the hawthorns and landed on the fire. 'Silly beggars,' said Robbie, 'we'll have to light it again.'

A moment later the corrugated iron shuddered and clanged beneath a rain of half bricks. The noise was deafening. There was dust in my mouth and through the bolt holes I saw the bricks, red and purple with jagged edges that could rip my flesh, bouncing over the bed of the gulley. I flattened myself to the ground, heedless of the damage to my cloak. I tasted blood and realised that I had bitten my lip. One of the bricks had punched a hole in the corrugated iron and I saw the sky glaring through it like blue enamel. 'Don't be daft,' shouted Robbie. 'Give over.'

There was no reply. The fire outside flared briefly then subsided into a smudge of thick yellow smoke that oozed into the drum and made our eyes water. I felt my heart pounding. Something had gone wrong with the game. It was not being played according to the rules which Robbie had spelled out. A flake of corrugated iron swung free on a hinge of rust and fell on my hand like a leaf. There was a trickle of dirt down the side of the cliff as though someone had crawled to the edge for a closer look, then the bricks rained down again. I curled into a ball and waited for the din to stop. The silence, when it came, was almost as frightening. I heard a lark spinning itself into the sky on a thread of song. I was aware of dust drizzling down the sides of the drum, forming mounds like miniature graves at the base. The wind blew between the layers of corrugated iron and shook them gently.

'Come out, both of you,' shouted someone.

It did not sound like Roy or Edwin but they were there, standing at the edge of the marlpit, surrounded by eight or ten bigger boys, and as we climbed out of the drum I realised what had happened. They had been taken prisoner by the estate gang. Their hands were tied behind their backs and Roy's air-rifle was resting on the shoulder of the biggest boy who wore long trousers and had a sheath knife strapped to his belt.

'Stay there,' he called. 'We're coming down.'

We watched them gallop towards us down the near-vertical cliff, whooping and shaking their fists, more terrifying than Indians or Riffs, fiercer than we were, boys who threw apple cores at the screen at the Palace and cheeked the manager and who claimed the marlpit as their own. At least, part of it. There was enough room for everyone, but certain spots – like the gulley with the metal drum – were more highly prized than others and it was not the first time we had been warned off. The boy holding Roy's air-rifle was named Brian Price. His father, it was rumoured, had been to prison and it was no use any of our parents complaining to him. Father and son were allies in a war in which we were the natural enemies.

'What are you avenue snots doing here?' demanded Brian.

'Just playing,' said Robbie.

Brian Price aimed the gun at his chest. 'I could put a bullet in you,' he said.

Robbie shook his head. 'It's not loaded.'

'Oh, no?' Brian Price pointed the rifle to one side and squeezed the trigger. A piece of shale starred and disintegrated and he snapped open the gun and inserted another slug. 'He had them in his pocket,' he said, jerking his head towards Roy. 'Didn't he say?'

'I'm not surprised,' said Robbie.

'He's not surprised! Don't he talk posh.' The estate gang sniggered. 'And look at this one,' he said, prodding me in the stomach. 'What's this little nancy got on?'

They crowded round, fingering the buttons of my cloak. 'ROSW,' said one of them, spelling out the letters. 'What's that mean?'

'It's my school,' I said. 'It's the initials.'

'Initials for what?'

I stared straight ahead. 'Royal Orphanage School Wolverhampton.'

'Orphanage!' said Brian Price. 'Are you an orphan?'

'Sort of.' I could not be certain, but I thought I could detect a slight softening in his manner. I had noticed it before when people encountered the word. It did not always disarm them, but it made them hesitate as if they had been introduced to a species to whom they owed a measure of consideration. It had affected me just as powerfully when I had seen it for the first time on the board outside the school. Orphans, I had been taught to believe, were less fortunate than the rest of us. They had no one to protect them. Their clothes were patched. They lived on scraps. It made me feel shabby and resentful but there were times when it was better to be pitied than bullied. It was not the moment to point out that some orphans were privileged and arrogant and confident that the rest of the world was inferior. It was an occasion for meekness and guile.

'What d'you mean, sort of?' he persisted.

'My father's dead and my mother's ill,' I said. 'She's lying up at home now.'

'Are you having me on?'

'No, I'm not. You can ask anyone.'

He jabbed Roy Greaves with his own rifle. 'What do you say?'

'It's true. His mother's been laid up for ages.'

'What's wrong with her?'

'She had an operation,' I said. 'She made medical history.'

'What are you talking about?'

'They operated on her brain,' I said. 'It was an experiment. They had to guess what they were doing. She nearly died.'

I could sense that the mood had changed. They were still in control and we were still their prisoners. But the urge to punish and hurt us had been deflected. In spite of themselves their imaginations were gripped. The temptation to see how much further I could take them was irresistible. 'It's still touch and go,' I said. 'The doctor comes to see her most days. She has these tablets that can kill you if you take too many.'

'What are they called?'

'It's a long name,' I said. 'Pheno something.'

'Pheno's Fruit Salts,' said one of the gang.

No one laughed and I felt my spirits lift. 'She's expecting me back. She said I wasn't to be out long.'

Brian Price rested his hand on the hilt of his sheath knife and looked at us each in turn as though what he read in our faces would decide what he did next. I recognised the pose. I could almost guess what he was thinking. The moment had come for a gesture which would show that even a brigand had a sense of honour. It was what Robin Hood would have done and Brian Price could do no less. He drew his knife and cut through the string that bound Roy's and Edwin's wrists. 'Hop it,' he said. 'And don't come back.'

'What about my rifle?' said Roy.

'You have to pay a ransom.'

'How much?'

Brian Price rubbed his chin. Having shown mercy he could afford to be a proper brigand again. 'Five bob.'

'I haven't got five bob.'

'All right, what have you got? Turn out your pockets.'

Between us we could raise three shillings. He counted out the silver and coppers in separate piles. 'I'll have that cap too,' he said to me.

'It isn't mine.'

'Let him have it,' said Robbie.

'And the bayonet.'

Edwin sniffed miserably. 'I'll tell me mam.'

'And what'll she do?'

'She'll have the bobbies on you.'

Brian Price plunged the bayonet into the ground. 'Not for this she won't.' He plucked it out and put the tip to Edwin's throat. 'What you've got here is a dangerous weapon. It's against the law. You say a single word about having something like this and you're in trouble.'

'It was my uncle's,' said Edwin. 'He had it in the army.'

'He's not in the army now.'

'Let him have it,' Robbie told Edwin. 'There's no point in arguing.' He turned to Brian Price. 'Can we go then?'

It was man to man, leader to leader. 'We'll count ten then we're coming after you,' said Brian Price.

'Twenty,' said Robbie. 'Be fair.'

Brian Price scratched his initials in the earth with the bayonet. 'Twenty,' he agreed. 'Get going.'

We raced across the marlpit and scrambled up the far side. By the time we had reached the top the estate gang was in pursuit. The pins securing my cloak flew out and as I ran I felt the skirt flogging my ankles. I tripped over a length of barbed wire buried in the grass and heard something tear. Robbie hauled me to my feet and we ran on across the broken tarmac where the lorries parked, past the Michelin man goggling down from the garage wall and into High Lane. We were safe. The estate gang would not follow us there. We paused to draw breath and I saw that my cloak was yellow with marl and had a three-cornered rip just below the belt. I poked my finger through the hole and stared at it, appalled by the damage. I thought what my mother would say and the exhilaration of our escape drained away to form a chilly pool in the pit of my stomach.

'They can mend it,' said Robbie.

'It'll show,' said Edwin. 'We should tell the bobbies.'

'You can brush off the muck,' said Roy. He dusted the stock of his rifle and blew down the barrel. 'Anyway, they didn't get this.'

'That's ninepence you owe me,' said Robbie. 'You've got to pay us back.'

We straggled homewards along High Lane. I considered calling into my Aunt Jenny's to confess what had happened, but as we approached the house I saw Mrs Aarons at her gate. She clasped her hands to her chest. 'My life!' she exclaimed. 'What have they done to you?' She grabbed Robbie's jacket. 'Was it you?' she demanded. 'Did you get him in this state?'

Robbie struggled free. 'It was the lads on the estate.'

'They should be arrested. Criminals!' Mrs Aarons pulled me towards her front door. 'We must clean you up. Your mother shouldn't see you like this.' She waved the others on. 'You go home. I'll see to him.' She drove me into the house and shut the door behind us, slipping the catch and shooting the bolt as though she expected my attackers to invade her sanctuary. 'Take off your coat,' she ordered. 'Such a mess you're in.' She saw the rip and, as I had done, poked her finger through the material. 'And this is your uniform. Your aunt told me. See what they've done. What will your mother say?'

The tears I had been holding back burst through and in Mrs Aarons' living room, with the artificial logs pulsing beneath the make-believe ash, I told her all that had happened, how I had smuggled the cloak out of the house, how we had been ambushed and robbed and made to run for our lives. She held my hand, gasping at each new outrage, her chest heaving, the scent of her body mingling with the salt that streamed down my nose. She hugged me fiercely and again I was aware of the ribbing beneath her dress. When she squeezed me I heard cords creaking like a tent tugged by the wind. The door opened and I saw a small boy standing in the passage. Imperiously, Mrs Aarons beckoned him towards us and gathered him in her embrace. Our heads collided and we stared into each other's eyes as we were rocked backwards and forwards in the swell of Mrs Aarons' emotions. 'This is England,' she moaned. 'That this should happen in England.' She stood up abruptly, still gripping our arms. 'You listen,' she said, shaking us to emphasise each word. 'You stay away from that place. You play where it's safe.' She let us go and straightened her dress, plucking it back into shape, smoothing it over her hips. 'This is Lennie,' she told me. 'He's a good boy. He does as he's told. He listens to his mother.' She smoothed his hair fondly, winding his dark curls around her fingers. 'You should think of your own mother,' she said. 'I told you already. You should think of her before you do these things.'

'I didn't know what would happen,' I whimpered.

'God gave you brains. You should use them.' She clapped her hands together as though she was dusting off a film of flour. 'All right,' she said. 'No more tears. Let's see what's to be done. The coat can be mended. We can wash your face. We can give you a glass of tea. Then we can take you home.' I tried to protest but she shook her finger sternly in my face. 'No arguments. Not another word.'

I thought for one fearful moment of what my mother would say when I arrived on the doorstep with Mrs Aarons, then I closed my mind to the subject. The worst had already happened. There was no sense in worrying about it. I found myself looking forward to the glass of tea.

Ten

MRS AARONS took my cloak to the invisible menders and she and my mother rejoiced over the neatness of the repair. 'How much was it? You must let me pay,' said my mother, reaching for her purse.

Mrs Aarons held up her hand like a policeman stopping traffic. 'For a friend, nothing.'

'But I insist.'

'Insist all you like.' Her generosity was implacable, a sunny wall in which there was no breach, and my mother acknowledged defeat.

It was a notable surrender, made more remarkable by the fact that after being hard pressed to make small concessions my mother gave ground at such a rate that, within days, Mrs Aarons found herself the sole freeholder of my mother's friendship.

'She's kindness itself,' my mother told me. 'I've never known anyone like her.'

The real distinction was that Mrs Aarons was unlike my aunts or anyone among my mother's contemporaries. She did not criticise. She did not reproach. She drew no comparisons. She thought my mother was brave, self-reliant, deserving and put-upon and frequently told her so. My mother was an example, she said. If we all tried to be like her the world would be a better place. My mother sat back, an audience of one applauded by the cast. I was not as outraged as Mary or the rest of my family. I knew the speed and the violence of my mother's changes of mood. I had seen her exasperation when her affairs were taken out of her hands and I knew that, although no one had actually blamed her for her inability to manage her health or her finances, she felt somehow at fault. She had been enraged by what she at first termed Mrs Aarons' charity. But to endure it she realised that she had to welcome it, accepting it as her due. She had never found it difficult to receive a compliment. She had been a pretty girl, a popular young woman and she had married a man many years older than herself. All her life she had been assured that she was attractive, companionable and loved and it required only a small shift of attitude to see Mrs Aarons as the latest member of her retinue by right. The degree of admiration was unusual, but my mother put it down to Mrs Aarons being a foreigner of sorts, new to the customs of the country.

What she warmed to was her vigour. After bringing me home, minus my cloak which she had spirited away to be cleaned and mended, Mrs Aarons had telephoned the police who had interviewed Brian Price, reclaimed Edwin's bayonet and returned our money. Everything was accomplished within twenty-four hours, although the re-telling of the story went on for several days. For the rest of the holiday I was assigned to Mrs Aarons as her errand boy, companion to Lenny and courier whose principal duty was to speed between our two houses with messages and gifts which ranged from jars of marmalade to bundles of women's magazines in which Mrs Aarons had marked passages she thought would be of special interest to my mother. Sometimes they were recipes, sometimes hints on how to utilise scraps of soap by moulding them into a multi-scented block, but most often they were inspirational paragraphs endorsing hope and fortitude, printed as prose but revealed to be verse when they were read aloud.

We learned something of the Aarons' family history. There were branches, it seemed, all over the world. Her parents lived in Manchester. She had relatives in Austria and Germany. An older brother had emigrated to America and established a business as a dealer in precious stones in Los Angeles. In Germany, she said, terrible things were happening. There had been arrests, property had been seized. The letters she received were upsetting because they were full of hints rather than facts. 'They don't want to frighten me,' she said, thumping her chest. 'But I know, I know!' Worse was to come, she prophesied. There were camps in Germany which no one dared talk about. People disappeared. No one was safe.

My mother poured her another cup of tea. 'But what about the police? If people are arrested there must be a reason.'

'The police!' Mrs Aarons tossed her head back and emitted a bark of laughter, like a dog demanding to be let out. 'They're not like the police here. They're not after criminals. They *are* the criminals. There's no mystery why people are arrested. They are Jews.' She stirred her tea so recklessly that it slopped into her saucer. 'Believe me,' she said, 'it is the start of the whirlwind. We shall be blown away. All of us, whoever we are.' She leaned across the table and gripped my mother's hand. 'Here too. When I saw your boy with his face muddy and his coat torn I saw him as one of my own. Like my own son. Like Lennie.' She sat back in her chair and shuttled the rings on her fingers like beads on a counting frame. 'Let me say this. When the time comes there will be a place for him with me. In America.'

'In America?'

'We have decided,' said Mrs Aarons. 'That's where we are going. Not this year, not next. But soon. My brother's finding a place for us.' She dug me in the ribs. 'Nice for you. Sunshine, oranges, movie-stars. Nice for your mother too.'

'For me!' My mother smiled tolerantly as if she had been offered a trip to the moon. The idea was too absurd to take seriously. 'I couldn't go there. Not for want of asking. I have a brother in Trenton, New Jersey. He's begged us to go, but there's no point in thinking about it.'

'You should think about it,' said Mrs Aarons, 'while there's still time.' She finished her tea and settled the cup neatly in the saucer. 'Mind you,' she said, 'Trenton is not Los Angeles. You don't have the sun.'

The matter was allowed to drop for that afternoon, but my mother referred to it several times during the next few days. She had been intrigued by the thought of going to America, impossible though it was. But she was puzzled by the urgency of the invitation. 'Germany's a long way from here,' she said. 'I don't see why she's so upset. Nothing's going to happen.'

'Mrs Aarons says it's already happening.'

My mother looked at me as if I had either misheard or

misunderstood the entire conversation. 'Only to Jews,' she said.

It was as though by becoming her friend Mrs Aarons had undergone some kind of conversion, which was not religious but social. Although she was undeniably Jewish, the fact was never referred to. When she mentioned it herself it was made light of or treated with the brisk compassion usually reserved for a disability such as Mary's missing finger or Mr Mason's cataracts. She could not be held responsible for what she was and politeness decreed that it should be overlooked.

'She's vulgar,' said my Aunt Ada, 'but she has a good heart. There's no denying that.'

Everyone agreed that she had shown remarkable initiative in taking my cloak to the invisible menders. The tear could scarcely be seen. The day before I returned to school my mother examined it for the hundredth time, marvelling that the damage could be so completely restored. 'You're a lucky boy,' she said. 'Lucky to have friends like mine.'

I did not want to go back to school. The prospect of meals in the dining hall, lessons with Mr Smith and Saturday afternoons spent shivering loyally on the touch-line while the house team was pounded into yet another defeat filled me with unutterable gloom. To add to my misery I had developed a rash on my chin which the doctor, on one of his visits to my mother, diagnosed as impetigo.

'Highly contagious, of course,' he said. 'I doubt whether they'll want him back till it's gone.'

My mother took a different view. My case was packed, the taxi was ordered and on an April afternoon I found myself stumping mutinously around the lawn waiting for it to arrive. 'Don't kick the grass like that,' said my mother. 'You'll dirty your shoes.'

'Who cares?' I muttered.

'I care,' said my mother sharply. 'So should you. And stop picking your chin.'

'It's getting worse. They'll put me in the infirmary.'

'Rubbish,' said my mother. 'Take me round the garden. There's some daffs coming up by the rockery.'

Bad temper on my part was all that was needed to

provoke in her a good humour so defiant that I could almost see it being brandished like a sword from its scabbard. Sometimes when I sulked she would sing to me one of her favourite songs, stressing the first word of each line and beating the time on my wrist as though I was an infant into whom the message had to be physically drummed.

> 'I *want to be happy*,' she sang
> But *I can't be happy*,
> Till *I've made you happy too*.'

I was not amused, nor was I when in answer to my asking what there was for tea she would sing a verse from the oratorio 'Judas Maccabeus' which began 'Oh wait and see how gracious the Lord is'. This was followed by a reminder that Patience was a Virtue and that All Good Things Come to Him who Waits. No framed samplers hung on our walls, but maxims abounded. My mother could be relied on to find one appropriate for any occasion.

The taxi arrived and we embraced on the front step. 'I don't want to go,' I wailed for the last time.

'Go on now,' said my mother, 'and remember this. Everyone's in the Same Boat.'

I pointed to my chin. 'They've not all got impetigo.'

'It's just a little rash,' said my mother. 'They won't worry about that.'

She was mistaken. Matron took one look at my face and consigned me to the isolation ward. It was a small room in the furthest wing of the infirmary. There were six beds with identical blue and white counterpanes. A single light hung from the centre of the ceiling and the floor glittered with wax. 'Get into bed,' said matron, 'we don't want you making the place untidy.'

'But I don't feel ill.'

'I'll decide whether you're ill or not. Heaven knows what they thought they were doing sending you back to school with your face in that state.'

'I told my mother,' I said.

'A pity she didn't listen,' said matron.

I looked round the bare room. 'Can I have something to read?'

'I'll see what I can find. If it comes in here it has to be thrown away afterwards. That's what isolation means.' She turned back the counterpane on the nearest bed. 'You can see the street from here. You won't feel so shut away.'

There was a view of the street corner and several back gardens. I saw trees leaning over fences, their branches thick with bursting buds, and flower beds one after the other like chevrons on a sleeve, patched with primroses. 'We've got daffs coming out in our garden,' I said.

'That's nice,' said matron. 'Don't dawdle now. I'll find you something to read, I promise.'

I undressed and got into bed and within half an hour she was back with a tray on which there was a plate of biscuits, a glass of milk and bound volumes of *Punch* and *The Quiver*, dated 1903. I studied pictures of ladies with their hair piled high like cottage loaves and men in striped blazers having accidents in punts and the real world receded still further. I heard sounds which I could identify – the clash of cutlery from the kitchens, the shudder of a desk being dragged across a floor, the slam of a window being shut – but they were all reduced like scale models, noises from Lilliput. I watched a flock of starlings settle in a tree opposite. They lined the branches, keeping a precise distance from each other, fluting and gargling until, at a signal which I could not detect, the chorus stopped and the birds huddled within their feathers as they prepared to roost.

No one knew I was in the infirmary, I decided. I was a prisoner in a tower, abandoned by the world. There had been no chance to report to Mr Smith. I still had my case and my clothes. As far as my friends and the school was concerned I had vanished without trace. At seven o'clock a maid brought me a bowl of soup and a plate of cold meat and salad. She had bright red hair and a pattern of freckles like rust across her nose. 'Matron says it's lights out at eight,' she said. 'She'll come and settle you down then.'

'What's your name?'

'Amy,' she said.

'Do you know Doris in the kitchen?'

'I'm new,' said Amy. 'This is my first job.'

'Do you like it?'

'I don't know yet, do I. They're a bossy lot, that's all I know.'

'Who's bossy?'

'All of them. That Nurse Tanser. Thinks she's Lady Muck, she does.' She drew a deep breath and strutted across the room, sticking out her chest. 'Come along girl, we've not got all day,' she mimicked. She pointed to a small window curtained with gingham, set in the wall behind the door. 'You'll see. That's her room. She'll be keeping an eye on you.'

I looked at the window with mixed feelings. It was cheering to know that I was not alone at the far end of the infirmary, but I did not enjoy the prospect of being watched.

'Not that she'll bother much,' said Amy. 'She's got better things to do.'

'What sort of things?'

'Never you mind,' said Amy. 'Nothing for you to worry about. You eat your supper and don't spill that soup on the sheets.' She tucked a napkin into my collar. 'Go on, before it gets cold.'

I was not hungry. I flushed the slices of cold meat down the lavatory and felt homesick when I read the inscription on the bowl. It had been made in Burslem. I knew the pot-bank, less than a mile from Uncle Ernest's house. We had walked past it beside the canal; my uncle, my cousin Jessie and her brother Ken, all of us with our eyes fixed on the yellow water, eager to be the first to see a fish ring the surface. My uncle awarded sixpence for the first sighting, but usually he saw the fish before any of us and claimed the money himself.

At eight o'clock matron came in to plump out my pillow and straighten the sheets. 'The doctor will see you tomorrow,' she said. 'I expect he'll prescribe some ointment.'

'The purple stuff?'

'I should think so,' said matron. 'Have you said your prayers?'

'Just before you came in,' I lied. The purple ointment was disgusting, a mixture which blotted the face indelibly like a birth mark. If that was to be the treatment I was glad to be in the infirmary until it was over.

Matron switched off the light and stood for a moment in the open doorway. 'Sleep tight,' she said, just as my mother did.

'All night,' I replied, completing the spell.

She closed the door and I lay in the dark with my eyes open. I stared at the window and tried to count the stars but before I had marked those filling one pane I fell asleep. When I awoke it was darker still, but a diffused light was shining through the gingham that curtained Nurse Tanser's window. I heard her laugh. Then I heard a man's voice, flat and gravelly and familiar. I got out of bed and crawled across the floor on my hands and knees. A cold draught blew up my nightshirt and goose pimples erupted silently between my legs. I raised myself cautiously until my eyes were level with the window and peered through the gap between the curtain and the window frame. Nurse Tanser sat on a leather pouffe by the gas fire, her shins rosy in the reflected light. Opposite her in a small tub chair sat Mr Smith. He had a cigarette in one hand and in the other a flask from which he was filling two glasses. He handed one glass to Nurse Tanser and picked up the other himself. 'Chin-chin,' he said.

'Cheers,' said Nurse Tanser.

Mr Smith crossed his legs and I saw that he was wearing patent leather pumps. 'Quite a decent band,' he said, not really addressing Nurse Tanser but letting the words float above him as if he had blown a smoke ring.

'Decent for here,' she said. 'At least they kept proper time. I can't bear it when they get the tempo wrong.'

'Nor me,' said Mr Smith. 'No point to it if the tempo's wrong. It's the same with cricket.'

'With cricket?'

'It's all rhythm,' said Mr Smith. 'You have to get into the swing. You can feel it in your bones when it's going right.'

Nurse Tanser sipped from her glass. 'That's how I feel about dancing.'

'I can tell,' said Mr Smith. 'You've got that natural flow.' He lowered himself on to the floor and traced the line of Nurse Tanser's calf with his finger. 'Streamlined,' he said. 'Beautiful.'

She caught his hand and held on to it. 'You'll spill your drink.'

'Not me.' Mr Smith's red face split into a fond grin. 'Never drop a catch, never spill a drop. Rules of the game.'

Their hands locked on Nurse Tanser's ankle and I could see their faces in profile against the glow of the fire. It was like the cover of a song sheet, I thought. Then without warning Nurse Tanser stood up and Mr Smith overbalanced. So did his glass. 'I'd better get a cloth,' she said.

'Don't go.' He reached after her as she whisked away into another, smaller room. The light went on and I heard the sound of running water. 'Frightfully sorry,' he said. 'Let me do it.'

'I can manage,' said Nurse Tanser. Her voice was very crisp and when she reappeared, a flannel in her hand, I ducked out of sight. For a count of ten I crouched with my chin resting on my knees, then I crawled back to bed.

The voices went on intermittently in the next room, but I could not distinguish the words. I heard Nurse Tanser's door open and shut loudly and the unmistakable clack of Mr Smith's feet down the corridor. Another door slammed and the footsteps receded. I slipped out of bed and peered through the window again. Nurse Tanser stood staring at the fire, her hands gripping the mantelpiece. After a while she unbuttoned her dress and stepped out of it when it slid to the floor. I watched as she plastered her face with cold cream and wiped it off with blobs of cotton wool, pausing between each stroke and studying her face in the dressing-table mirror. It was as though she was erasing the details of a pencil sketch. Her eyes became smaller, the line of her lips less precise. She smoothed her eyebrows and plucked out a stray hair from either side with a pair of tweezers. She put out her tongue and examined the reflection. She bared her teeth and turned her head from left to right, rotating the grin like an ornament.

I knew that I was spying on a ritual that should be completely private. I wanted to step back from the window, afraid that I would be seen but even more afraid that by leaving I would miss further revelations. Nurse Tanser raised her right arm, then the left and studied each armpit in turn. She rolled down her stockings and stroked her legs, not as Mr Smith had done but clinically as if it was part of a standard procedure in which she was both doctor and patient. She was so absorbed that even when I pitched forward slightly while changing position and banged my forehead on the glass, seconds passed before she looked in my direction. I leaned back into the shadow and she did not see me, but she was suspicious of whatever it was that had disturbed her. She scooped up her dressing gown and as she struggled to put it on I scrambled into bed and pulled the blanket over my head. The door of my room opened and I heard Nurse Tanser pad across the floor and stand beside me.

She peeled back the blanket as deftly as she would have removed an adhesive plaster. 'Were you by the window?' she demanded. I buried my face in the pillow and groaned. My heart was pounding and I was certain she would hear its fearful tattoo. I felt her hand on my shoulder. 'Are you really asleep?' I sensed that she was far from certain and ploughed more deeply into the pillow. 'Just let me catch you, that's all,' she said. I did not stir until I heard both doors open and close and the rustle of the curtain as she tugged it into position. Minutes later her light went off and I imagined her watching the same window that I had watched, trying to decide what I had seen. The school clock struck twelve and I thought of Mr Smith barging his way through the dormitory, uprooting radio earths and aerials as he strode unswervingly to his corner cabin. The starlings in the tree opposite gave a concerted shiver as the clock tolled on, then sank back into sleep. I rehearsed the letter I would write in the morning. 'Dear Mother,' I began. 'I am in the isolation ward. I told you I should have stayed at home with my impetigo.' It was no great consolation being able to prove I had been right, but it was only just that my mother should know she had been wrong.

I stayed in the infirmary for two weeks, bored and apprehensive, my face jammy with purple ointment. Nurse Tanser never referred to the night I had spied on her through the observation window, but her curtain remained tightly drawn and several times when she took my temperature, my pulse jumping under her fingers, I felt she was appraising me, wondering how much I understood and what gossip I was likely to repeat.

I had understood nothing, but everything I had seen I described to Carpenter as we sat together in the boiler cage. He pressed me for further details. 'Was it just her dress she took off?' he asked.

'And her stockings.'

'Stockings don't count,' said Carpenter. 'What I mean is, you didn't see her nude.'

'Not what you mean,' I said, thinking of Nurse Tanser's armpits, as bare as a plucked chicken.

'What about Smithy? You're sure all he did was stroke her leg?'

'They held on to each other,' I said. 'He held her leg and she held his hand.'

'Were they having a row?'

'Not what you'd call a row. They weren't shouting or anything. He just banged the door when he left.'

'Smithy always bangs doors,' said Carpenter.

'Mostly when he's fed up.'

Carpenter edged away from the boiler and rubbed his thigh where it had been scorched by the hot metal. 'Why do you think he was fed up?'

'He didn't want to go,' I said.

'He was rejected!' Carpenter raised a knowing finger. 'His advances were repulsed. Tanser gave him the push.' I envied the ease with which Carpenter wrote his scenarios, basing them, more often than not, on the flimsiest of evidence. But his sketch of the episode I had witnessed seemed both credible and likely. When we saw Mr Smith at his desk the next day he had the look of a lover who had been scorned. We took note of his short temper, his pink eyes and his restlessness and we understood. Luckily, though, his unhappiness had no adverse effect on his cricket. In the first match of the term he captained the juniors against the seniors and scored a century. It was not a match which had lasting significance – by the time we played the return the teams had altered – but for twenty-four hours it was pleasant to be on the winning side.

From the regularity with which Carpenter returned to the subject of Nurse Tanser I realised that I had been granted a unique experience. Carpenter never said as much, but almost every day he coaxed me into repeating what I had seen through the window. 'Pity you bumped your head before she was nude,' he said. It was one of his favourite words. He held it in his mouth, savouring the taste, before releasing it and gradually the sense and sound formed an image in my mind. I pictured a nectarine, juicy and smooth-skinned and I could see why Carpenter envied me. He had magazines with photographs of nude women, but none of them were equal to my imaginings. They all seemed to be keen on games and the open air. They were photographed swimming and playing tennis and tossing large beach-balls to each other. Often they were standing in bracken or beside low shrubs whose branches forked across their bodies like leafy bunting. When their bodies were not covered by leaves or tennis rackets or beach balls, they seemed extraordinarily hairless. Studying the area below their waists it looked as though each had been tacked into position on the page with a large, blunt thumb which blurred every detail.

Carpenter rolled up the magazines and stowed them behind the boiler. He hugged his knees and rocked backwards and forwards, a reliable sign that an idea was taking shape. 'Tanser's too risky,' he said. 'We'll have to try the girls' dorm.'

I looked at him blankly. Carpenter had a habit of announcing his plans when they had reached their final stage, leaving out not only ways and means but also the object of the exercise. 'What about the girls' dorm?' I asked.

He drew two parallel lines in the dust on the window sill and chopped them into three sections. 'First section, our dormitory,' he said. 'Middle section, clock tower and sewing room. End section, girls' dormitory. The same loft runs above all three sections. There are ventilators in the ceilings. If we get up there we can see through.'

The proposition still seemed incomplete. 'But what is there to see?'

'Girls undressing,' said Carpenter, as though he was making it plain to an idiot.

'Who else is coming?'

'No one else. Just you and me.'

'Have you done it before?'

'Others have,' said Carpenter. 'There's a door in the clock tower. Five minutes to get up to the loft. Five minutes there. Five minutes back. There's nothing to it.'

He was right as usual; the plan was put into operation that night. We waited for two hours after lights out, then put on our trousers and plimsolls and slipped through the baize door at the end of the dormitory, past the sewing room and into the clock tower. There was a flight of steps which led to the striking mechanism and the clock face, but half-way up the stairs was a door, no bigger than the lid to a locker, through which Carpenter crawled and pulled me after him. He wedged it slightly ajar with a fragment of lath which he pulled from the roof. 'We don't want it slamming shut while we're still up here,' he said.

He shone his torch down the length of the loft. There was a carpeting of dust as dense as fur, but beneath it we could plainly see the outlines of the beams on which we had to crawl. Carpenter put his lips close to my ear. 'Be as quiet as you can. We don't want them to hear us below.' He looked left and right, making sure of his bearings. 'It's the senior dorm over there. Follow me.'

He gripped the torch between his teeth and crawled forward at a steady pace. The beam was broad enough to walk on, but there was plaster on either side and I visualised myself bursting through the ceiling like a chick emerging from an egg. It was safer to stay on all fours. We passed one ventilator which threw a faint glow on to our faces as we hung over the grille. I could make out a row of beds in which rows of sleeping girls lay, their faces dusky beneath the night-light. Carpenter beckoned me on. 'That's the way,' he said, pointing to a small spur on our right.

Voices filtered through the ventilator, eddying upwards like threads of cotton caught in a draught. I felt as though I was absorbing them through my hands and knees. Only the ceiling separated me from the bodies below. It was like eavesdropping on miners who were going about their business, ignorant of children at play over their heads.

Carpenter pointed silently to the grille and I followed the direction of his finger. A tall girl with her hair tethered by a ribbon stood by her bed. She took off her gym slip and folded it over the back of a chair. Then she removed her vest, then her navy blue knickers. Crouching almost directly above her I could see the parting in her hair and the bumps on her chest. She pulled a night-gown over her head and they disappeared.

'Well, then,' said Carpenter. 'What d'you think of that?'

I thought of Nurse Tanser's bosom swelling secretly beneath her starched white apron. I thought of Mrs Aarons creaking beneath her black silk like a ship heeling into the wind. I thought of the nudes in the magazines and Carpenter's determination to see what was to be seen and I did not wish to sound ungrateful. 'I've never seen anything like it,' I said truthfully.

Carpenter shone the torch beneath his chin and grinned like a gargoyle. 'You know what's so good?' he demanded, squatting on the beam as if he was hatching a vital discovery. 'It's not that they're pretty. They're not, all of them. What matters is that girls are different from us. Completely different.'

I saw the moon through a loose tile and poked my finger through the gap to feel the night air. I knew that I had been presented with a fact of life more interesting and more important than anything I would learn as part of the school syllabus or delivered impromptu by Mr Sleath. Carpenter had discovered the truth for himself and while he could not explain it he was prepared to pass it on for me to examine and hold and value. The understanding would come later, I decided. 'You're right,' I agreed. 'They're completely different from us.'

Eleven

THAT SUMMER something extraordinary happened to time. I had always imagined it as a beach on which waves incessantly built and demolished their green walls, where the horizon was further away than you could see and the long view was entirely natural. A day there could expand to infinity; sometimes fruitfully, sometimes uneventfully. Hours were elastic. Not only did they go slowly. It was possible to halt them altogether, holding them fast while they absorbed sensations like a balloon breathing in gas which would ferry it over country yet to be explored.

Suddenly the process quickened. Weeks and months were telescoped. Days rippled by like the teeth of a comb strummed by my finger. I was late for everything; behind with my prep, last in the relays, marked absent from the register seconds before I burst into the classroom. I forgot to write home and my mother complained to the headmaster. One morning at assembly after we had sung the hymn and listened to the scripture reading Mr Gibbs took an envelope from his pocket and placed it on the lectern. 'This,' he said, 'is a letter written to me by an exceedingly distressed mother.'

He paused to allow his words to take effect. Boys studied their neighbours, heads in the front rows swivelled round, there was a subdued trill of interrogation. 'I shall not name the boy,' said Mr Gibbs. 'He himself knows the anxiety he has caused. His mother is an invalid lady, housebound and alone. She relies on his weekly letters for news and as a lifeline to the world outside. But for five weeks he has not written to her.' There was a buzz of outrage and he raised a finger. 'She has sent urgent messages, begging him to write. But he has chosen not to respond, so in desperation she has written to me.' He held up the envelope and I recognised the stationery. I felt my face turn red and stared at my shoes.

'As you all know,' said Mr Gibbs, 'an hour is set aside every Sunday afternoon for you to write home. If any of you lack stamps or writing paper, all you need do is ask and they will be provided. There is no possible excuse for this kind of neglect. Cruelty.' My cheeks burned and I heard myself panting. I wished myself miles away, anonymous and hidden. I thought longingly of a toy I had once been given, a deep-sea diver in a sealed jar, who went up and down when I pressed the lid. I had studied his face, muzzled like a dog behind his diver's mask, and thought I recognised myself. He touched bottom. He rose to the surface. He made his journeys in public, but his identity remained private. Time, too, was on his side. The pressure was remote; he was suspended between now and then, concealed by his diving suit, guarded by water.

Mr Gibbs rapped the lectern and, unwillingly, I raised my head. He was looking straight at me. Everyone could see. 'What I want this boy to do,' he said, 'is write home today. Immediately. He will report to me after this assembly and answer this letter.' He lifted the envelope again and waved it like a flag whose signal I could not fail to recognise. I stared at his purple face trying to ignore the scrutiny of those who peered at me like an animal in a cage. 'Very well,' he said. 'School dismissed.'

He waited until my row had begun to file out of the hall, then he beckoned me towards him. 'You should be ashamed of yourself,' he said.

I concentrated on the floor, seeing, as if for the first time, fillets of new wood which had been let into the worn boards. Behind me I heard the hall empty. My fingers tied themselves into greasy knots. '*Are* you ashamed?' asked Mr Gibbs.

'Yes sir.' My voice was less than a whisper.

'I can't hear you. Speak up.'

'Yes, sir,' I said.

'Don't you love your mother? Don't you know how worried she is?'

I nodded silently, praying for an excuse, fluent and irre-futable, which would allow me to escape. 'I meant to write, sir,' I said. 'I was interrupted.'

'For five weeks? You were interrupted five times?'

'No sir.'

'I should think not,' said Mr Gibbs. 'Don't be absurd.' He stepped down from the lectern, plucking his gown into shape and strode down the aisle without a backward glance. 'Come along boy,' he said. 'Don't dawdle.' I followed him, trotting to heel, along the corridor to the door of his study which he unlocked and motioned me inside. He pointed to a table by the window on which several sheets of school writing paper lay beside the pen and ink. 'Sit down,' he said. 'Commence writing. In forty-five minutes time I expect you to have completed two pages.' He took out a watch from his waistcoat pocket and showed me the dial. 'There will be no interruptions,' he said, 'and there will be no more excuses.'

I dipped the pen in the ink-well. 'Dear Mother,' I began, 'I am sorry I have not written sooner.' I was not in the least sorry I thought. What I felt was rage and dismay that I had been betrayed. It was true that I had not written. I knew that my mother was worried. But in complaining to Mr Gibbs she had broken faith. She had become one teacher enlisting the help of another. I recognised the alliance and the futility of protesting against it. I had no defence, no weapons which were of any consequence. The pen-nib bucked on the paper when I pressed down on it and a fine spray of ink spattered across the page. I blotted it and wrote more carefully. I listed my progress in form, my introduction to cricket, the theme of the previous week's essay but I left out any item of news which would indicate what I was truly feeling, whether I was happy or sad or sorrier than Mr Gibbs told me I ought to be. I wrote to the end of each line. I left no gaps and I did not cheat by filling up the final inch with rows of kisses. I signed the letter with much love and gave it to Mr Gibbs to read. Only twenty minutes had passed since he had showed me his watch.

He held the letter at arm's-length as if he was studying a score, frowning slightly when he saw the ink blots. He decided not to mention them. 'You see,' he said, 'you can do it if you try. You can do it if you try. You can write an excellent, informative letter which any mother would be delighted to receive. Why on earth didn't you do it in the first place?'

I hung my head and said nothing and he rapped his knuckles on the desk. 'I want an answer.'

I tried to think of some way in which I could explain how time had slipped its leash and was racing ahead of me while I stumbled breathlessly behind, trying to catch up. It was no good, I thought. Even as I rehearsed them the words sounded foolish. 'I forgot, sir. I did start to write, but I forgot to finish.'

Mr Gibbs covered his eyes with one hand as if the light was too strong. He remained blinkered for some time and when he took his hand away his expression was only mildly incredulous. 'Fascinating,' he said. 'Have you heard of the condition known as amnesia?'

'No sir.'

'From the Greek,' said Mr Gibbs. 'It is a state of mind. Or rather a state of no mind. At a guess I would say it is what afflicts you.' He watched me stamp and address the envelope and indicated a tray on his desk. 'Leave it with me. And Oakes . . .'

'Yes sir.'

'Make an effort in future. Remember to remember.' He waved me to the door. 'Back to your classroom. Don't dawdle.'

Dawdling was not allowed. It frayed moral fibre. It encouraged idleness. It was the antithesis of all that Mr Gibbs stood for. I realised that, in his own way, he was as preoccupied with time as I was. He hated to waste a minute. His classes started the moment the period bell had ceased to ring. He read and answered his mail before breakfast so that his correspondence would not invade other parts of the working day. His singing engagements were miracles of planning, with hire-cars taking him to the studio or concert hall at a precise time and bringing him back with equal promptness. He could not, he often declared, bear hanging about. It was one degree worse than dawdling because it was usually the fault of another party and consequently beyond his control. On a day when all his arrangements worked as he intended he found it possible to combine a full stint of teaching with a broadcast, usually from Birmingham, in the morning or afternoon and a recital at night. Even when his programme was less busy than he would have wished he still contrived to give the impression of being on urgent business, speeding from one part of the school to another to make spot checks on damaged text books, graffiti which had appeared on the wall of the Blacking Shed, the cigarette machine in the entrance hall which had been plundered overnight, forbidden comics discovered in the dormitory. Usually he made his rounds with Mr Sleath in tow, his nose reflecting the tint of the headmaster's cheeks, a large notebook at the ready to take down any dislocation of the norm which caught Mr Gibbs's eye. He was a devoted Boswell, recording not only the facts of the complaint but also the exclamations uttered to describe it.

Scraps of food found under a table in the dining hall would be listed, in Mr Gibbs's words, as a 'disgusting mess'. Toilet paper littering the floor of the lavatories would be set down as 'frightful squalor'. Telling us, as he frequently did, of the headmaster's devotion to duty Mr Sleath would read passages from his notebook, reciting them like poetry, declaiming them like texts. He sought to inspire us with the same zeal that they awoke in him. 'You boys don't know how lucky you are to have a head like Mr Gibbs,' he reminded us. 'Night and day he's at it. Day and night. I give thanks for such a man. On my knees.' He placed his hand on his notebook as if he was taking an oath. It was not necessary. We never doubted Mr Sleath.

It was he who first investigated the outrage of the locker room. The phrase was, as usual, coined by Mr Gibbs. But unmistakably Mr Sleath shared his anger. So, by the end of a week, did the rest of the school.

The locker room was where we kept small personal belongings which we used from day to day. It was situated between the quadrangle and the classroom; a big, bare hall lined with cupboards, each bearing a blue and white enamelled plaque stamped with our school numbers. The floor bristled with splinters. In front of each window there were radiators on which we sat, roasting our hams in winter, cooling our legs in summer. The heat, we were told, was bad for us. 'Tha'll get chinkoff,' Mary warned me when I described the luxury of finding a seat there in frosty weather. She would not elucidate further but chinkoff, I gathered, was both painful and embarrassing. 'Just you think on,' she said darkly. 'If you get it, you'll know about it.'

We used the locker room as a meeting place. There was a notice board on which details of film shows and sports fixtures were pinned, but there was no other decoration. Originally the lockers were painted brown, like paupers' coffins. The summer term, however, brought a surprise. An old boy had donated several hundred pounds to have the locker room refitted and when we returned to school after the holidays we found it flanked with cabinets of pale oak, each door fitted with brass numerals and brass handles which echoed the bright grain of the wood. It was slightly intimidating. Everything was so clean that we were afraid to touch in case we left a mark. The timber smelled of vinegar as if each board had been lightly disinfected. The walls seemed to give off a faint radiance. 'It is a magnificent gift to the school,' Mr Gibbs told us. 'You will show your appreciation by treating it with consideration and respect.'

No one disagreed. The lockers became an accepted part of the school furniture and nothing more was said until one morning, three days before half-term, Mr Sleath bustled into the dining hall where we were having breakfast and clapped his hands for silence. He waited until every sound had died away, then climbed on to a chair by the top table. 'Can you all hear me?' he enquired. 'Very well then. Pay attention. I have just come from the locker room. Someone has defaced one of the lockers. Naturally, the headmaster will have to be informed, but before I make my report I want whoever was responsible to come forward.'

He paused and looked hopefully up and down the tables. No one moved and Mr Sleath shook his head. 'I'm disappointed. I really am. I expected better.' He surveyed us all like a king rejecting a rabble of unworthy subjects, then dismounted from the chair and without another word swept from the hall.

The silence held until the door closed, then there was an

instant buzz of conversation which grew to a roar. 'What's defaced mean exactly?' asked Fisher.

Carpenter tapped his head with a tea-spoon. 'Don't be dozy.'

'Spoiled,' said Minton. 'Like drawing whiskers on a picture.' He nudged Carpenter. 'What have you been up to, then?'

'Don't blame me,' said Carpenter. 'I don't know what he's talking about.'

'Tell us another.'

Carpenter returned the nudge, just as Minton had picked up his cup of tea. 'I mean it,' he said. 'Don't give anyone ideas. This could be serious.'

None of us guessed how serious it was to become. We packed the locker room after breakfast to inspect the damage. On the wall of the locker nearest the quadrangle someone had gouged the crude outline of a sun, a lopsided circle with rays shooting out from it like the spokes of a wheel. 'It's not much,' said Fisher. 'It's only a scratch.'

Carpenter traced the pattern with his finger-tips. 'Wait and see.'

His forebodings were justified. Morning assembly began us usual. We joined in the hymn. Mr Gibbs read the lesson, then shut the bible with a bang. 'Let us pray,' he said. It was not an invitation but an order and the prayer was not one of the headmaster's brusque man-to-man chats with the Almighty, but a fitness report on the entire school which found us wanting in every respect.

'O Lord,' said Mr Gibbs, 'we are Thy unworthy servants, guilty of the most base ingratitude. We honour nothing: not our parents, not our teachers, not our benefactors. We are indolent, devious and greedy. We complain that we are ill-served, but what is given to us gladly we waste. We squander our opportunities and our portion. We neglect the chance to make ourselves better men. We are ignorant and improvident. We sin in the darkness and conceal our wrongdoing.'

I watched Mr Gibbs secretly, squinting through my fingers as his prayer gathered power and momentum. His hands gripped the lectern on either side. His head was thrown back and his face was suffused with colour. His neck bulged over his collar like dough rising in a warm room. It was how he looked when he was singing one of his more boisterous ballads. 'Lord,' he said, 'we ask Thy guidance. We beg Thy mercy. There are those among us who would let others suffer for their wickedness. We beseech Thee to counsel them wisely. Speak to them Lord. Enter their innermost hearts. Advise them through Thy servants. End their night of doubt and let them wake with clear eyes.' He yearned heavenwards, as if trying to direct his words into some divine ear, only to fall back, anchored to earth. 'Amen,' said Mr Gibbs.

His address to us was more direct. 'Mr Sleath has already spoken to you regarding the outrage of the locker room,' he said. 'I can only hope that the majority of you are as disgusted as I am. It is vandalism for which there can be no excuse. I regard it as an insult to the entire school, an act of desecration for which every boy present must bear responsibility.' His colour, which had ebbed slightly, began to rise again. His voice shook as though someone was tugging his ankle. 'One boy, or several boys committed the act. Others must know that he committed it. It is not only contemptible behaviour. It is criminal. And it will not be tolerated.'

He released the lectern and threw out his hands as if he was tossing crumbs to sparrows. 'I am determined to know who did this thing,' he said, almost conversationally. 'If the culprit has any sense of honour he will come forward, as Mr Sleath has already invited him to do. If he does not come forward it is the duty of anyone who knows his identity to tell me.' He smiled grimly at the murmur of surprise that stirred the hall. 'Some of you are thinking of the code of honour that has always been a tradition here. But it does not apply. I am not asking you to sneak on a friend. He is not your friend. What he has done has offended us all. He does not deserve your loyalty.'

For the rest of the day, gangs of vigilantes roamed the school, pinning suspects in corners and quizzing them until they burst into tears. Carpenter came through his cross-examination unscathed. 'I told them,' he said. 'It's not the *sort* of thing I do.'

The prefects formed themselves into a squad of gentle-man investigators commandeering a corner of the library where they debated the incident under the headings of motive, opportunity and method. They decided that a com-pass had been used to incise the locker, although the irregular shape of the sun argued against it. The most likely motive was thought to have been boredom. Even less helpfully, they concluded, everyone in the school had an opportunity of committing the crime.

Mr Sleath played detective too, beginning with a break-down of the previous twenty-four hours – listing who had been in the locker room, however briefly and for whatever reason. His list grew unwieldy. There was no one who had not passed through the locker room at some time during the day. Several boys, it transpired, had dodged PT by hiding in the changing room which was directly opposite the locker which had been defaced. Mr Sleath's manner became elaborately offhand. 'So you were looking for something to do,' he suggested.

'No sir.'

'But you must have been. You had over an hour to kill.'

'Not really sir.'

'What were you doing then?'

'Playing cards sir,'

'For money?'

There was scarcely a moment's hesitation. The perfect alibi had presented itself. 'Only for halfpennies, sir.'

'Gambling,' said Mr Sleath, writing avidly in his note-book, burying one crime with another. 'I shall report this to the headmaster.'

'Yes, sir.' Their relief was like a fanfare.

At the end of the day the mystery was still unsolved. We returned again and again to the locker, staring at the scratches as though they would yield the vital clue which would point to the culprit. 'Maybe he did it left-handed,' said Fisher.

'How could you tell?' asked Minton.

Fisher considered the question. 'Experts could tell.'

'Call for Sherlock Holmes,' said Carpenter.

At assembly the following morning Mr Gibbs told us how

he proposed to deal with the matter. 'The vandal has not come forward,' he said. 'Nor has anyone found the courage to reveal his name. I cannot believe that the guilty person is unknown to at least some of you. Someone is protecting him. Therefore the responsibility is yours.' He pointed to the calendar hanging below the clock on the wall. 'Half-term begins on Thursday, which is the day after tomorrow. There is, I believe, a full programme of cricket and athletics and a film show on Saturday evening. Unless, by Thursday morning, I have the name of the boy who defaced the locker none of these events will take place. Instead, you will spend the time standing in line in the locker room. You will assemble by houses. You will not read. You will not speak. You will take your meals in silence. Then you will continue to stand until someone has the sense or the decency to tell me what I wish to know.'

We listened to the sentence like condemned men. We were appalled by its injustice and depressed by what appeared to be its inevitability. There was no likelihood of anyone confessing to the locker room outrage. The crime and its consequences had become atrocious. Even if someone confessed, the headmaster's punishment would be nothing compared to the recriminations of the school he had put at risk. What struck me as perverse was that Mr Gibbs's decree was designed to cause him considerably more distress than his pupils. He valued time more highly than we did. It pained him to see it go to waste. Time was more than money. It was lumber which could be made beautiful, fallow land which would yield a crop. Time spent in the locker room was dead time. Even while I hated him for devising such a discipline I knew how sick at heart he must be.

All that day and the next the vigilantes increased their pressure. There were ambushes in class rooms. Wrists were seized and the Chinese Burn applied. Several boys had their heads jammed down lavatories and the chain pulled. Tucker came to visit me at night. 'Don't worry,' he said. 'I won't let them get you.'

'I didn't do it,' I said.

'They don't know that. They don't care.' He put his arm round me. 'I care what happens to you,' he said.

Mr Smith made his own attitude clear. 'As far as I'm concerned it's just a scratch on the side of a locker,' he said. 'I don't care who did it, or why. All I know is that it's likely to interfere with certain plans I had for the next few days and if it does I give due warning to whoever's responsible. I'll cripple him.'

On Thursday morning we filed into assembly, still hoping for a reprieve. It was not granted. 'No one has come forward,' Mr Gibbs informed us coldly. 'There is nothing further to say. You will go from here to the locker room.' It was almost an anti-climax. We filed down the corridor and paraded in houses between the banks of lockers, blond beneath their varnish, of which the headmaster was so proud. House captains tidied us into ranks, the smallest to the front, taller boys to the rear. I estimated that there were over three hundred people standing in line. Talking was forbidden, but there was a wordless colloquy of coughs and sighs, one side of the room answering another, those at the front hacking painfully until there was a bronchial response from a friend somewhere behind. Through a window to my left I could see a small square of the headmaster's garden. The sun shone on new grass and apple blossom. Clouds like billows of whipped cream sailed across a patch of sky. My feet began to ache and I tried putting my weight first on one leg, then the other. I studied the neck of the boy standing in front of me. He had the beginnings of a boil where his hair became bristles. In the three days we stood in line I saw it grow red and angry, chafed by his grubby shirt. On the last day he covered it with a plaster.

The school captain had the job of supervising the parade with a small army of prefects as his lieutenants. At the start they tried to make it a military operation, patrolling the ranks with their hands clasped behind their backs, their expressions uniformly stern. Their only diversion was to try and locate the source of the occasional whisper or intercept notes which were passed from hand to hand. Names were taken, lines imposed. But gradually the novelty wore off, the policing became lax. We discovered ways of surreptitiously reading comics, hiding them under the flaps of our blazers. Several rows away from me two boys played chess on a pocket board. I tried to write poems in my head. I remembered the plots of films I had seen and re-invented the dialogue. At lunch on the second day Carpenter claimed that he had learned how to sleep standing up. 'What you do is concentrate on a spot on the wall,' he said. 'You have to try and put your mind there. You don't need to close your eyes. You just float away.'

Masters paid us regular visits and I understood why Mr Smith had been so aggrieved when the ultimatum had first been delivered. The plans by which he had set so much store had been aborted and, like it or not, he was on duty. His red face glowered as he came through the door and he swaggered resentfully up and down the room, kicking his feet as if the air itself was in his way. He raised his head and sniffed. 'This place stinks,' he said loudly. 'Open some windows.' For ten minutes he led us in deep-breathing exercises, only a little disconcerted when a boy standing in front of him fainted and collapsed on his well-polished brogues. 'It's all right,' he said. 'No one else need move. I'll get him to the infirmary.' He gathered the body in his arms and clattered away in the direction of Nurse Tanser.

The headmaster came to see us morning and afternoon. He was attended by Mr Sleath who stood behind him, his hands clasped across his notebook, his head cocked to one side when Mr Gibbs spoke, like the terrier in the gramophone advertisement. There was no hope now of discovering who had defaced the locker. We knew it; so did Mr Gibbs. The investigations had failed. So had the appeals to our collective conscience. So, in the last resort, had the punishment. But still it went on. It was like watching the progress of a colossal boulder which had been launched down an incline, crushing everything in its path until the ground levelled and its wild career slowed to a steady trundle, less menacing but impossible to stop until it had run its course. The damage continued, painfully and pointlessly, inch by inch. There was still ground to cover; still time to be served. On Saturday morning we began to count the hours that remained. At five o'clock Mr Gibbs told us that we were dismissed. No one moved and he told us again that we were free to go.

'Didn't you hear me?' he snapped. 'I want this room cleared.'

There was still no response. We stood chained by a weary patience which made us indifferent to his disgust. It was less than mutiny. It was barely resistance. The locker room had been our jail for three days; now it was ours by right.

Nothing more was said, no orders given. Mr Gibbs turned on his heel and marched through the door which Mr Sleath bobbed forward to open. He rounded the corner and as the sound of his footsteps dwindled and died a sense of relief rinsed through the room. I felt myself rising like the diver in the bottle, freed from pressure. Carpenter grabbed my arm and spun me round in a leg-flailing polka. I heard myself cheering. We were all cheering. We ran out through the quadrangle and into the playground, giddy as if we had just been roused from hibernation. Five minutes late, the school clock chimed and we stopped in mid-stride to listen. I wondered if Mr Gibbs was listening also, counting the beats, measuring the waste of time.

At the end of term there was an extra item on the school bill. Below the charges for haircuts and shoe repairs there was a levy of two shillings, my contribution towards the cost of a new locker. There was also an explanatory note. 'Parents are requested not to pay this sum themselves,' said the final paragraph. 'In the circumstances I would prefer the cost to be borne individually by each boy.' It was signed in red ink: 'Geo Gibbs. Headmaster.'

Twelve

THREE YEARS LATER the locker room outrage was still remembered. Several parents – although my mother was not among them – refused to pay the headmaster's levy and, as if to reproach the defaulters and remind us that the crime was still unsolved, Mr Gibbs left the defaced locker as it was. Dirt sank into the scratches. The wood itself mellowed. In time the buckled sun became one of the sights of the school. Visitors were taken to see it, along with the initials 'JB' carved on the wall of the clock tower dated 1900, and a flaw in one of the dormitory windows said to resemble the face of the founder.

It was like returning to the site of a battle in which we had spilled blood. Those of us who had stood in line for three days saw ourselves as veterans whose wounds still ached in wet weather. We reminisced about the campaign and agreed that there had been giants in those days. The new breed of juniors were a weedy lot.

It was imperative that year not to be weedy. War was still unimaginable (or rather, it was not as we imagined it), but we all felt that we were about to be tested. Every day the newspapers carried photographs of troops on the march, of people waving flags and horses drawing gun carriages. Mr Gibbs attended meetings of the Territorials in full uniform, his riding boots burnished, his Sam Browne glowing like a spar of mahogany across his chest. We were issued with gas masks which stank, said Carpenter, like old farts. The vegetable garden in front of the art room was dug up and two concrete air-raid shelters were sunk in the soil between the runner beans and the cabbages. They smelled of disinfectant and water seeped through the walls to form pools on the floor. They were swept out regularly but the water always returned. Each shelter was two-tiered. The top bunk was simply a long hammock made of hessian tightly stretched over a wooden frame. A nick with a pen-knife started a rip like a ladder in a stocking, which decanted the sleeper on to the boards below. There was room in the shelters for every boy and every member of the staff, said Mr Sleath. We were not likely to need them, but it was better to be prepared.

He was appointed Chief Warden, responsible for organising the air-raid drill which, if our timing measured up to Mr Sleath's demands, was intended to spirit us from any part of the school to the safety of the shelter within three minutes. It was an ambitious target, but Mr Sleath let it be known that he meant business. Like Mr Gibbs he had preserved his uniform from Flanders. To prove to us that he had once been a military man accustomed to mounting operations, he displayed it, complete with campaign ribbons, on a home-made dummy in the art room. But all that he took from it to equip himself for his new role was his steel helmet which he painted white and inscribed with a large black 'W'.

No warning was given when the drill was to be called. A hooter, newly installed in the clock tower, sounded the alarm, braying frantically and incessantly until the last straggler had checked in to his bunker. The day-time drills disrupted lessons. The night-time drills fragmented sleep. 'Walk, don't run,' said Mr Sleath, checking us as we pelted along corridors and down fire escapes. 'Broken legs lame more people than shrapnel.' Sometimes, if he felt the routine was becoming stale, he would have us swarm down rope ladders pitched from the dormitory windows. The knack was to lean back with your shoulders and press your feet hard against the wall, but on my first descent I panicked and found myself dangling by my fingertips watching the dawn lighten the sky behind the school chapel. It glowed like a coal, a hint of the fire to come.

Apart from the air-raid drills there was no change in the school curriculum. In geography lessons we coloured maps of Germany, shading the coal-bearing region of the Ruhr with black crayon. In biology I gouged a hole in half a potato and as water rose mysteriously in the pit I had dug I learned the principle of osmosis. Preparations went ahead for Sports Day. I was entered for the long jump, the hundred yards and the half mile, besides which I was chosen for the choir which was to lead the entire school in a programme of songs conducted by Mr Gibbs. They included 'The Mermaid' (in which Mr Gibbs was the soloist), a Gilbert and Sullivan selection and 'Non Nobis Domine'. We rehearsed every day, except Saturdays and Sundays, for a month. Our rehearsals were the only times we could be sure we would not be interrupted by air-raid drills. Sometimes as we sang Mr Sleath appeared at the back of the music room, his white helmet strapped under his chin, a clip-board which had replaced the notebook in order to accommodate a deluge of government pamphlets, tucked under his arm. He never interrupted, but sat patiently, his helmet glimmering against the oak panels until Mr Gibbs paused for breath. Then he would clear his throat and almost surreptitiously march forward and make his report. It was as though he was indulging the headmaster by allowing him to pursue his hobby while his loyal servant contained the crisis.

Mr Gibbs conducted in his shirt sleeves. Perfectly round beads of sweat appeared on his forehead as if it had been squeezed like orange peel and he mopped it with a coloured silk handkerchief which hung half out of his hip pocket. He taught mathematics to the senior boys and geography to the juniors, but music was the only subject which he seemed to take actual pleasure in teaching. He urged us to enjoy the exercise. 'To sing is to make a joyful noise,' he declared. 'Let me hear joy in your voices.' To encourage us he laughed up and down the scale, guffawing into our faces as if to make us inhale his enthusiasm. Close up he looked drunk. A gold tooth gleamed in his open mouth. His thinning hair which had come ungummed in the heat of the rehearsal shook as if it was stirred by a fan. His eyes bulged. He placed our hands on his belly so that we could feel the notes vibrate. It was like standing on the edge of a railway platform which began to tremble as the train approached.

For the final week we rehearsed in a marquee which had been put up in the top playing field. It was striped red and white like a circus tent and at one end there was a piano and a small stage. The songs sounded very different under canvas, smaller and lost in the grass-scented twilight. 'It will be different again with an audience,' said Mr Gibbs. 'Don't bellow. Make them listen.'

There was no chance of my mother attending Sports Day. Her headaches were becoming more frequent and intense, besides which she now suffered from what she called 'her attacks' when, without warning she fell down and foamed at the mouth. Aunt Jenny took me to one side and explained that it was something the doctors termed *petit mal*. It was not as dreadful as it looked, she said. But excitement brought it on and my mother would not risk making a public exhibition of herself. Her paralysis had worsened and her left leg was swollen like a balloon filled with water. She hated her appearance. 'I know people are looking,' she said. But earlier in the term Mrs Aarons had persuaded her to let them drive her to visit me. The car protected her from unwelcome stares. She managed to climb the short flight of steps at the school entrance and when I was called out of class to see her, she was sitting at the back of the assembly hall, a travelling rug wrapped about her legs, with Mrs Aarons beside her.

Our conversation was stilted. I told her about the programme of songs we had been practising and, fearful that someone would come in and hear me, sung a verse from each while she leaned forward, her eyes fixed on my face.

'Beautiful,' exclaimed Mrs Aarons, applauding softly with her hands snug in black kid gloves.

'Sing me some more,' said my mother.

I hung my head. 'I can't remember any more.'

'Of course you do,' said my mother. 'You must. You'd not be in the choir otherwise.' She turned to Mrs Aarons. 'He gets it from me, you know. I was singing solos when I was his age.'

I sang a verse of *'Non Nobis Domine'* and Mrs Aarons gave me a box of peppermint creams. 'For a good boy,' she said.

'You'd better make the most of them,' said my mother. 'Mrs Aarons won't be with us when you come home.'

The peppermint dissolved on my tongue and I licked my lips. Mrs Aarons' sweets were always better than any we could afford to buy ourselves. 'Where are you going?'

'I told you,' she said. 'America. There's a song you should be singing. You know the one I mean?'

'I don't think so.'

She winked gaily and beat time with her plump little hands. To my horror, she began to sing. 'California, here I come. Right back where I started from.' She stopped and smiled. 'In a manner of speaking, of course. That's where we'll be living. You remember me telling you? My brother's fixed us up. Sunshine and oranges. A swimming pool, even. We sail next week. Mr Aarons and Lennie and me. All on the good ship lollipop.'

My mother squeezed her arm. 'I shall miss you.'

'And I shall miss you, my darling,' said Mrs Aarons. 'I shall miss you all.' She dabbed her nose with a lace handkerchief. 'You're my very best friend. I'd take you with me if I could.'

My mother let go of her arm. 'There's no chance of that.'

'So you say. But you never know.' She rolled her eyes meaningfully. 'Times change. Things happen. Just remember, the mat says Welcome.' She embraced me and I heard the familiar creak of harness beneath her dress. For some reason it moved me more than anything she had so far said. We were joined in a moment of high emotion. I breathed the mingled scents of her clothes and her body and I knew for certain that it was for the last time.

Before they left to drive home Mrs Aarons took my mother to the staff lavatory and I went outside where Mr Aarons was pacing the drive beside his parked car. 'A fine building,' he said, grinding his cigarette end into the gravel.

'Founded in 1850,' I told him.

'So long ago?' He rubbed his hands together as though he felt a sudden chill. 'Nothing like that where we're going.'

'I suppose not,' I said.

'America is the New World,' said Mr Aarons firmly. 'Very efficient, they tell me.'

'Do the refrigerators work?'

'What do you mean, refrigerators? Of course they work.' He struck his forehead with the flat of his hand. 'What a memory. That old thing. We'll do better than that in California.' He took a pound note from his wallet and tucked it into my top pocket. 'Say nothing. Spend it in good health.'

He and Mrs Aarons saw my mother safely into the back seat of the car and tucked the rug around her knees. 'I'll think of you singing,' she said.

'I'll remember.' I knelt beside her as she flung her arms around my neck, then backed away grinning with embarrassment. Mrs Aarons kissed me again. Their departure seemed interminable. Behind me I sensed faces peering through the windows and I prepared my answers to the questions I knew would come. As the car crunched slowly down the drive I saw that both my mother and Mrs Aarons were crying and before they turned into the traffic I ran back into the school, slamming the door behind me.

'Was that your mother?' asked Carpenter.

'That's right,' I said. 'She's an invalid.'

'Which one?'

'She was sitting in the back.'

He nodded reflectively and accepted one of my peppermint creams. 'Who were the other people?'

'Just friends.'

'They had a posh car,' he said. 'They looked foreign or something.'

'They're going to America,' I offered.

'They're not American, though.'

'English,' I said. 'They live near us at home.'

'What's their name?'

'Allen,' I said. Mrs Aarons' kiss was still warm on my cheek and I felt like Judas.

'That's not foreign,' said Carpenter.

'Of course it's not. I told you they were English.'

Carpenter put out his tongue and squinted down at the chocolate that coated it. 'Some people just look foreign,' he said. 'It isn't their fault.'

My mother sent Mary to come and cheer me on Sports Day. She arrived before lunch, in time to see me win the long jump for the under-twelves. 'I did eleven foot six,' I told her as she knotted the sleeves of my sweater round my neck.

'That's a fair distance,' she said.

'Better than fair.'

'Listen to him,' she said to no one in particular. 'Who's blowing his own trumpet then?'

'I am,' I said. 'Just so you'll know I want an ice-cream.'

Mary bought us both vanilla tubs from the Stop Me and Buy One tricycle that was parked outside the playing field gates. 'Your mother gave me the money,' she said as she peeled off the lid and dropped it carefully into the litter basket. She was wearing the same outfit that she had worn the day she first brought me to school. The glass cherries chinked on her hat and I could see the small gilt safety pins that secured her modesty vest to the front of her dress. She wagged her wooden spoon at me. 'Don't you spoil your appetite.'

'Don't you either.'

'You'd best not tell your mother you had ice-cream before your lunch. She'd skin us both.'

Mary was enjoying herself, I could tell. She sat on the bench beside me, kicking her legs. Sunlight filtered through the leaves. In front of us races were being run, javelins thrown. The marquee stood four-square, striped like candy. Mr Sleath was wearing a steward's badge in his lapel. He had abandoned his helmet for the day, but the whistle he used to urge us on in our drill still hung round his neck, a badge of office he was loath to relinquish. In the refreshment tent, close to the cricket pavilion, the cook decorated plates of ham with posies of lettuce leaves, shrouding them with a vast white table cloth. Mr Smith strolled by, his buckskin boots immaculate, his flannels perfectly pressed, the collar of his shirt turned up at the back. He seemed about to stop, but in mid-stride I saw him scan Mary from head to toe and he nodded briefly and passed on.

'Is that one of your teachers?' she asked.

I scraped round the bottom of the carton gathering the last of the ice-cream. 'That's Smithy. He's our form master.'

'He's very smart.'

'Not up here,' I said, tapping my forehead.

'That's not polite.'

'Neither is he.'

She giggled happily and I saw her easing off one shoe with the toe of the other. Buried in the branches above our heads a loudspeaker coughed and I heard Mr Sleath's voice, solemn as always when he was on official business. 'Ladies and gentlemen, may I have your attention,' he said. 'I have an announcement. The headmaster does not wish to interrupt the day's arrangements but he believes you would like to be kept informed of the progress being made in the attempts to rescue the submarine *Thetis*.'

Mary's shoe fell off but she ignored it. There was a rustle of paper and Mr Sleath's voice continued. 'The BBC has just broadcast a bulletin saying that the salvage vessel *Vigilant* is standing by and an air line has been attached to the submarine. That is all we know at present, but we will keep you informed of further developments. Thank you.' There was a loud click as the speaker went dead and a ragged burst of cheering, like a roll of caps exploding sporadically one after the other, echoed round the field.

I threw the ice-cream carton in the air. It was exciting to share in a drama which we all knew would end well. I had read about the *Thetis* in the morning paper. It was a new submarine undergoing its diving trials somewhere near Liverpool. Something had gone wrong with the machinery and, for the time being, it was stuck on the sea bed while battleships and cruisers steamed to its aid. It was vaguely connected with the talk of war, but unlike other news items about troops on the march and politicians meeting for talks which no one understood, it was clear-cut and exhilarating. Men's lives were at risk, but it was simply a matter of time before the Navy did its job and they were rescued.

'You'd never catch me going down in one of those things,' said Mary.

'They'd never fit you in.'

'Cheek,' she said, swatting me with her programme.

The sports were timed to finish at four o'clock. We had half an hour to shower and change. The concert was due to begin at five, then there would be speeches and presentations. We joined Carpenter and his mother for lunch, eating our salad at trestle tables which had been set up in the cricket pavilion. The walls had been freshly white-washed and the sunshine coaxed out the keen smell of lime.

Mrs Carpenter had a long, lined face in which her powder

gathered like streaks of cement. She wore pearls and a pale linen coat and her straw hat had a veil hanging from the brim like a fruit net. 'I'm sorry that Mrs Oakes isn't well enough to be here,' she said, stabbing a radish on the rim of her plate.

Mary looked up from the tomato she was dissecting. 'She has to take things quietly. There's no sense in asking for trouble.' She had succeeded in removing most of the seeds, I noticed. If we had been at home she would have been peeling off the skin with her finger-nails.

'I shall write and tell her about everything,' I said.

Mrs Carpenter inclined her head. 'I'm sure you will.'

'He was told off about not writing,' said Carpenter treacherously.

'That was years ago.'

'What's that got to do with it?'

'Everything,' said Mrs Carpenter. 'It's part of growing up.' She hoisted Carpenter by his elbow and pointed to the serving table. 'I think we'd all like some fruit salad.'

'No strawberries for me,' said Mary. She leaned towards Mrs Carpenter and pointed to her open mouth. 'It's the pips, you see,' she whispered.

That afternoon I came second in the hundred yards and nowhere in the half mile. Later in the changing room Carpenter asked me what Mary had meant by refusing the strawberries. 'She has false teeth,' I said. 'The pips get under her plate.'

Carpenter feigned disgust. 'Pips under her plate! Do they grow there?'

I threw a flannel at him, soaking his clean shirt. In retaliation he turned on the cold tap and jammed his thumb under the nozzle, spraying the walls and drenching the floor. We heard the drum-beat of heels across the locker room and instantly ceased hostilities. 'When you're quite done,' said Mr Smith, flinging the door open. 'We've got visitors coming round here later on. You can stop playing silly beggars. Get off down to the marquee.' He grabbed Carpenter's collar as he hurried past. 'When it's all over you can clear this room up. I want it spotless. Do you understand?'

The sun had re-lacquered his face and it shone like scarlet tin. 'It wasn't only me, sir,' said Carpenter.

Mr Smith propelled him through the door. 'Don't argue with me. Just do as I say.' He followed us across the quadrangle and through the gate. 'You too, Oakes,' he called after us. 'You can give him a hand.'

In the marquee the choir had already begun to assemble and we took our places in their third row. Carpenter's voice was on the point of breaking, but we were still counted as trebles and in chorus we sang with the girls who had been co-opted for Mr Gibbs's recital. In front of us, separated by a hedge of hydrangeas, sat the governors and parents. I saw Mary near one of the exits. She disliked the heat and she was alternately fanning her face with her programme and dabbing her chest with a tiny handkerchief. Mr Gibbs announced the titles of the songs and nodded to Mr Griffiths, the music master, who sat poised at the piano. He struck a chord and the music surrounded me. I could see it like clouds, like meadows of sound. In 'Non Nobis Domine' it hemmed me in like cloisters. When we sang 'The Mermaid' I felt as though I was in the eye of the storm. The basses in the back row roared like the sea. The altos piped like the wind and we, the trebles, shrilled like jolly sailor boys, up-up-up aloft with the landlubbers lying down below. When I licked my lips I could almost taste the brine that coated them.

We sang it again as an encore and then sat as we had been told to sit, with our hands in our laps and our feet placed neatly together, while the house captains came up to the platform to receive the sports prizes and Mr Gibbs thanked the parents for coming and the kitchen staff for making such excellent provision for the day. I saw Mr Sleath sidle past the hydrangeas and wait until the headmaster came to the end of his address. He handed him a slip of paper and stood back, his face owlish in its gravity.

Mr Gibbs skimmed through what was written on the paper, then read it again more slowly as if committing the words to memory. For several seconds he seemed unable to speak and when he raised his hand for silence his fingers were trembling. 'Ladies and gentlemen,' he said, 'I have just received dreadful news. On such a happy day the tragedy is even more difficult to accept, let alone understand.' He studied the paper once more, then cleared his throat. 'It has just been announced that at three o'clock this afternoon the mooring cable attaching the submarine *Thetis* to the salvage vessel *Vigilant* broke and the submarine has sunk to the ocean floor. Rescue attempts are continuing, but it is feared that nearly a hundred lives have been lost.' Far away a lawn-mower bored through the heat of the afternoon. Mr Gibbs raised his head and looked out over the rows of faces. 'This Sports Day is over,' he said. 'It would be unseemly to continue in the light of events. Before we go, however, I would ask you to join me in prayer for those men whose lives are in danger.' He clasped his hands and closed his eyes. 'Our Father,' he said and we repeated the words, awed by the moment, eager to get to our crystal sets.

I walked with Mary to the tram stop. Her feet pained her and while we waited for the tram she took off one shoe and massaged the toes, flexing them gingerly one at a time. 'I should have worn my other pair,' she said. 'I can hardly stand.'

'You must take a taxi from the station.'

'Taxis cost money.'

'We never had that other ice-cream,' I reminded her. 'Not after Gibbo told us about the submarine.'

Cleaning up had begun within minutes of the announcement being made. Strings of bunting had been taken down. The trestle tables were stacked. Chairs were being removed from the marquee and I could see Mr Sleath slackening the guy ropes while a gang of men stood beside the contractor's lorry ready to dismantle the tent itself. The striped canvas was an affront; we were already in mourning. The tram swung round the corner and wheezed to a halt. I helped Mary aboard and watched it lurch away, sparks gushing from the overhead wires as it crossed the points. As I walked back to school I caught myself whistling under my breath. It was 'The Mermaid', the song we had sung so cheerfully that afternoon. But the melody was spoiled. The jolly sailor boys were no longer up-up-up aloft. Like the landlubbers they lay below, their lungs filled with salt water, while above them marker buoys jogged in the tide and rescue vessels tapped out their signals of no hope.

They were casualties of peace, Mr Gibbs told us at a memorial service the following week. But no one was deceived; every day the war crept closer. Air-raid drills took on a new meaning. Windows were measured for blackout curtains. Mr Granger, the master who had enrolled me on my first day at school, took part in a Saturday evening debate on whether or not human life was sacred and announced that if war was declared he would not fight. He had already registered as a conscientious objector.

An hour later someone had pinned a white feather to the door of his study and for the remainder of the term his classes were interrupted by a clear but undetectable chant of 'Conchie' which bounced like a random echo from one side of the class room to the other.

'I don't blame him,' said Carpenter. 'He's only doing what he thinks is right.'

'He's scared,' said Minton.

'How d'you know?'

'It's obvious. He doesn't want to get himself killed.'

'Who does?' said Fisher.

Carpenter removed a gob-stopper from his mouth and checked on the number of times it had changed colour. So far it had gone from red to green to orange which left only purple still to come. 'There are worse people than Granger,' he said, nodding towards the house beyond the top wall of the playground. 'What about them? They've done a bunk already.'

He was telling the truth. We had seen them go, watching from the dormitory window while furniture was loaded into a removal van and a woman in a green apron stowed china ornaments into the back of a Wolseley saloon. People were leaving the district every day. Everyone knew they would soon be making munitions in the factories down the road and if war came they would be obvious targets for the bombers. Mr Sleath told us in an unguarded moment that there had been a rush to buy country cottages in Wales. 'It's unpatriotic,' he said. 'Worse than that, it's scare-mongering.'

'We should go and see what they've left behind,' said Carpenter.

'You mean break in?' said Minton.

'Why not?'

'And pinch things?'

'Don't be in such a hurry.' Carpenter crunched the last of his gob-stopper, savouring the aniseed pip at its core. 'All I said was that we should go and see.'

'When?' asked Fisher.

Carpenter dug his hands in his pockets and surveyed the playground, damp and deserted after an evening shower. 'How about now?'

We followed him in single file through the vegetable gardens, hugging the wall of the top air-raid shelter and bending double as we crossed the patch of open ground in view of the art room. There was a light burning in Mr Sleath's office at the back of the building, but of Mr Sleath himself there was no sign. Carpenter scrambled up the wall that separated the school from the abandoned house and plucked at the single strand of barbed wire that lay across the top. It was frail with rust and came apart at his touch. He straddled the wall and motioned us to stay down until he had folded the wire back on either side.

'Now,' he said. 'One at a time.'

We hauled ourselves over the wall and lay in the long grass of the orchard. There was a carpeting of windfalls. The bigger apples had been mined by wasps and drowsy insects clambered over my hands. We crawled towards the house, keeping to the cover of the trees. A laurel hedge bordered the drive and peering through the marbled leaves we could see across the lawn and down into the school playground. The rain had stopped and one or two boys were playing a knockabout game of cricket. No one was looking our way. We circled the house on our knees, testing door handles and prising at windows. Quite unexpectedly one gave way, sliding upwards under the blade of my knife. We froze, half-expecting someone to shout, but the inside of the house was dark and hushed.

'I'll climb in and open the door for the rest of you,' said Carpenter. He flowed over the sill like water and waved us back to the side entrance. We heard the snap of a Yale lock and the rattle of chains and Carpenter stood in the passage beckoning us in.

There was a smell of damp and old fat as if a meal had been cooked and the windows sealed just before the owners left. We separated and prowled from room to room. In the master bedroom the bed was unmade and yellow silk sheets formed a puddle on the floor. Drawers hung open, shirt sleeves and strips of lace trailing on to the carpet. On a dressing-table there was a jar of Brylcreem sprouting green mould. Downstairs in the sitting room a cupboard opened on to a narrow passage which ended in a peep-hole through which, standing on tip-toe, I could see the front door.

'What was that for?' I wondered aloud.

Carpenter took a look. 'They were spies. Or gangsters.' The idea seemed to please him. 'If we pinch something it's not really stealing. It's probably loot already.' He took a cigarette lighter from the mantelpiece and gave it to me. 'It's a Thorens. Swiss-made. Put it in your pocket.'

He leafed through an array of birthday cards around which dust had already formed tiny earthworks. One of them had a shape cut out of the front fold which revealed the outline of a pair of breasts. Beneath them was printed the inscription 'You Dirty Dog'. I opened the card and saw that the breasts were, in fact, the haunches of a terrier squatting beside a large, spreading pool. I folded the card and the breasts reappeared. It was very strange, I thought. No one I knew would stand a card like that on their mantelpiece for anyone to see.

'Let's get back,' said Minton.

Carpenter chucked him under the chin. 'Who was it you said was scared?'

We were all whispering as though there was someone in the next room who might hear us if we spoke naturally. The light drained away and as we still foraged singly and in pairs we bumped into each other. I sat in the middle of the dining room floor and watched a bloody streak slice the sky from one side to another and it seemed like an omen. The house was suddenly oppressive. I wanted desperately to be outside.

I grabbed Carpenter's arm. 'I'm going.'

'Don't panic,' he said. 'I'm coming too.'

He shut the side door behind him and led us back behind the laurels, through the orchard and over the wall into the school garden. 'Now we separate,' he said. 'We'll meet in the boiler cage in ten minutes.'

Fisher and Minton returned the way we had come. Carpenter and I circled the woodwork room and sauntered openly up the front drive as if we had been to the school chapel. No one stopped us or spoke to us and we were first back in the cage. I examined the lighter which Carpenter had given to me. It was made of silver and had a small wheel on the front which operated a safety catch when it was turned to the right.

'They must be rich,' said Carpenter. 'How could you forget something like that?'

'The beds weren't made,' I said. 'They must have left in a hurry.'

Carpenter flicked the lighter and we watched the blue flame gutter and die. 'The petrol's run out,' he said.

'I can get some more.'

He hugged his knees and rocked himself backwards and forwards. 'What about that spy-hole?'

'Should we tell someone about it?'

'Don't be stupid.' He flicked the lighter and tried to catch the sparks. 'You want to hang on to that,' he said.

Weeks later we saw police in the grounds of the house. They had ladders and tape-measures and at morning assembly Mr Gibbs asked us if any boy had been over the wall. 'I am aware that it's not unknown for cricket balls to find their way there,' he said. 'No accusations are being made. The police simply want to know if there have been any expeditions in that direction.'

Carpenter and I looked straight ahead. 'I have already told the inspector I think it unlikely that any boy from this school would trespass on someone else's property,' said Mr Gibbs. 'However, if anything of the sort *has* occurred it is your duty to say so.' He passed on to other matters – the loss of school library books and the waste of soap in the ablutions – and I felt free to breathe again.

We circled the playground during mid-morning break and studied the house from a safe distance. The police had gone and curtains had been drawn across the windows as if someone had died. 'We say nothing,' said Carpenter. 'There's nothing useful we can tell them and we'd only get ourselves in trouble.'

Minton stared at the blind windows. 'But what d'you think happened?'

'They were spies,' said Carpenter positively. 'They got out just in time.'

'Where did they go?'

Carpenter grinned. 'Where d'you think? Germany, of course. Or America.' He dug me in the ribs. 'Wasn't that where those friends of yours were going?'

'That's right,' I said. 'But they weren't spies.'

'I never said they were. I only said they looked foreign.'

'They were British,' I said.

'But they were getting out too,' he insisted.

'I suppose so.'

The air-raid hooter started up and we walked rapidly towards the shelters. I thought of Mrs Aarons in the California sunshine with the oranges and the film stars and I remembered her telling us of the whirlwind that was on its way. I covered my ears as the noise increased, and began to run. I was glad that she was safe and I wished that she had taken me with her.

'What was their name?' asked Carpenter, trotting beside me.

I thought hard. 'Allen,' I said. 'There's nothing foreign about that.'

Thirteen

AT HOME the air-raid precautions were less advanced. My mother refused to apply for an Anderson shelter although the neighbours urged her to do so. 'I'll never be able to manage the steps,' she said. 'Anyhow, I don't want them digging up the garden.' Instead, she studied the leaflets which came through the letter box, advising us to equip a first-aid box with lint and bandages and ointment for burns and to cover every window with strips of brown paper to protect us from flying glass.

It was like getting ready for a picnic to be eaten indoors. There was a feeling of holiday on which the unexpected was bound to happen. On our last day at school Mr Smith told us he had volunteered for service with the RAF. 'So I won't be seeing you lot next term,' he said. 'I won't pretend I'm sorry.' He tilted his chair back and stared through the window, still with longing, but without the resentment which had punished him for years. Already he could see himself, spruce in his uniform, his cap at an angle, his tan contrasting with the blue of his Trubenized collar. 'I should have done it ages ago,' he declared.

Minton put up his hand. 'Will you be a pilot, sir?'

'There's no point in going otherwise,' said Mr Smith. 'You've got to get in early to get the good jobs.' He flattened his palm and flew it above his desk, diving down to strafe the blotter with a roar of engines and a hail of imaginary bullets.

'You'll be like Biggles, sir,' said Minton.

Mr Smith accepted the compliment. 'Very likely.'

'Have you been in a plane before, sir,' asked Fisher.

'Lots of times.'

'I mean have you flown one, sir?'

Mr Smith's good humour faltered momentarily. 'Of course I've not flown one. That's what I'm going to learn.'

He smoothed his hair and leaned back at an even more reckless angle. 'I'm not expecting any problems,' he said. 'I'm a very experienced driver. I've been round Brooklands.'

It was one of his proudest boasts that he had once driven a racing car for a bet. We had heard the story many times. 'I love speed,' he said, drawing a deep breath. 'I could have taken it up professionally.'

He had the chance now, I thought, lying on my back on the lawn at home while my mother poured soapy water on the greenfly that beaded the roses. It was one of the jobs about the house which she insisted on doing. 'You don't understand,' she said, when Mary protested. 'I can't bear feeling useless.' My mother's jobs included making the custard, chopping up bread and suet for the birds and drying out sections of orange peel on the hearth to use as firelighters. She also insisted on arranging the flowers and making the pot-pourri which she kept in a rose bowl in the front room. Its scent contrasted oddly with the balls of camphor which she stuffed down the sides of the settee to discourage moths. But it was useless to complain. 'I don't want them laying their eggs in there,' she said, stroking the plush of the three-piece suite. 'Good furniture costs money. It needs looking after.'

My Uncle Frank and Aunt Edna had invited me to spend part of the summer holiday with them at their home in Westcliff. They had a bungalow only five minutes from the sea and my mother insisted that I should go. 'Just think of it,' she said longingly. 'You'll be able to watch the breakers coming in.'

Through her eyes I saw waves breaking on rocks braided with sea-weed and gulls gliding over canyons of air. As she became increasingly housebound she dreamed of freedoms she had never known. She collected photographs of harvesters embracing sheaves of corn and gypsy caravans and Scottish crags. She spoke fervently of camp fires and hikes and the wind on the heath, and not to share her enthusiasm was to deny her the liberty she could only imagine.

'I wish you could come,' I said.

She folded her hands resolutely in her lap. 'Well, I can't. And that's that.'

'Uncle Frank's got a car. He's offered to drive you.'

'It's much too far.'

'We could stop off on the way.'

She shook her head violently as if she was afraid that I might persuade her. 'I've already told you. It's too difficult.'

'Stop going on about it,' Mary told me. 'Your mother's made her mind up.'

'I won't enjoy it,' I said.

My mother pinched my arm so sharply I yelped with pain. 'Indeed you will, my lad. Count your blessings and let's hear no more about it.'

I went to Westcliff the following week. My aunt and uncle met me at Euston and we had lunch in the station restaurant. I showed them my map of the journey with points of interest marked in red ink.

'Who gave you that?' asked my aunt.

'Uncle Arthur,' I said.

'He would,' said my Uncle Frank.

I studied him covertly over the restaurant table. Everyone in the family said we looked alike and I tried to recognise myself in his plump, slightly petulant face with its double chin that spilled over the knot of his tie. His fair hair had started to thin at the temples and his skin was the colour of lightly-done toast. He had worked on the Gold Coast for several years as a civil engineer building roads and bridges. My mother said he had been very good with the natives. 'They respected him,' she said. 'He never had anyone beaten unless it was really necessary.'

Aunt Edna was his second wife. His first wife, also named Edna, had died five years earlier and his remarriage to a much younger woman had been the subject of intense family debate. I remembered my Aunt Ada's disapproval. 'It's not decent,' she told my mother.

'I don't see why not,' she said.

'There's twenty years difference. That's why not.'

'But they seem very happy.'

'Happy!' said Aunt Ada, pursing her lips as if she had forgotten to add sugar to the rhubarb. 'What's happiness got to do with it? She's far too young for him. It'll come to grief, you mark my words.'

They looked happy, I thought. Aunt Edna had crisp brown hair which bounced below her ears as if it was on springs. She wore a pink dress level with her knees, and silk stockings in which her legs shone like new pennies. Between courses she studied her face in a round, silver-backed mirror and crayoned her mouth with lipstick. She ate very little, but encouraged me to stoke up on roast beef and new potatoes and then to order an ice-cream sundae for afters.

Uncle Frank sighed. 'They'll have to send out to Joe Lyons for it.'

'We're in no hurry,' said Aunt Edna. She smoked a cigarette in a long ivory holder, taking care to blow the smoke away from the table. When she brushed flakes of ash from the table cloth I noticed her nails, as bright as blood. No one else in our family used nail varnish. 'What do you want to do most of all on this holiday?' she asked.

'I don't mind.'

'We'll make a list,' she said. 'You can go swimming for a start. Or we can hire a boat. Or we could run down to Southend for the day.'

Uncle Frank sighed again. 'Little Palestine,' he said.

'There's the pier,' said Aunt Edna, taking no notice. 'People fish from the end of it. We'll buy you some tackle on the way down.'

I took my new purse from my pocket and counted out my money on the table. I had exactly ten shillings. 'Will that be enough?'

Aunt Edna squeezed my hand. 'I'll treat you.'

'Mother said I should pay for things myself.'

'She didn't mean fishing tackle.'

'How do you know?' I asked.

'We know,' said Uncle Frank loudly. 'Just put your money away.' He waved at the waitress and secured the bill. 'Joe must be making a packet,' he said.

'Who's Joe?'

'It's just a joke,' said Aunt Edna. 'Joe Lyons makes the ice-cream.'

'And charges for it,' said my uncle. 'It's an old Palestinian custom.'

I fell asleep on the way to Westcliff. When I awoke we were turning up a short tarmac drive towards the bungalow. It was festooned with honeysuckle. The front of the house was a sun porch and flowers hung over the windows like a bead curtain. The lawn was burned brown and bees droned over it, tripping over plantains and stalks of couch grass as they fumbled their way into heads of white clover. Beneath an ornamental cherry there was a ring of concrete toadstools and a small pond in which goldfish basked. All the houses in the road were bungalows. Some were hung with wooden shingles which the weather had turned silver like fish scales. Others were beamed and there was one with a thatched roof. They all seemed to hug the ground as if they were ducking continuous winds and the air smelled urgently of salt and tar.

'We'll have tea on the porch,' said my aunt. 'I'll just show you where you can wash first.'

I picked up my case and followed her through the front door, across a parquet floor and into the sitting room. All the curtains had been drawn against the sun and I stumbled over a leather hassock that I failed to see in the gloom. 'Here we are,' said Aunt Edna, opening two doors, on either side of a small passage. 'Here's the bathroom and this is your bedroom. Why don't you take off that pullover? You must be roasted.' I did as she suggested, then went into the bathroom to wash my hands and face. There was scented soap on a spiky rubber mat. The towels were looped through brass rings clasped in the jaws of lion masks set in the wall. On a glass shelf there was a jar of bath salts like green sugar and a drum of dusting powder which wheezed gently when I put the lid back on. The lavatory paper was soft and padded, unlike the stiff roll of Bronco we always used at home, and in the medicine cabinet over the basin there were scissors and tweezers and an implement made of orange rubber whose use I could not begin to imagine. When I combed my hair in the mirror I saw that the glass was tinted pink. It made my face look as though I had already caught the sun.

There were two teapots on the tray in the porch and a sliced lemon beside the milk jug. 'Indian or China?' asked my aunt.

'I beg your pardon?'

'Tea,' she said. 'Which would you like?'

'Give him Indian,' said Uncle Frank, 'boys of his age don't like China tea.'

My aunt lifted the smaller pot. 'He won't know unless he tries. He can always change his mind if he doesn't like it.' She smiled at me. 'Isn't that right?'

'I suppose so.'

They both watched me while I sipped the straw-coloured tea. It tasted of smoke and flowers and then of nothing at all. 'Look at his face,' said my uncle. 'Throw it away and give him the other.'

I held on to my cup. 'I like it.'

'Of course you don't,' said Uncle Frank. 'You don't have to be polite.'

'Honestly,' I said, 'I think it's very nice.' I tasted it again. 'I mean different.'

'It's certainly that,' he said. He leaned back in his canvas chair and put his hands behind his head. 'We thought you might come down in your uniform. It's very smart.'

'It's too hot,' I said, watching the lawn shimmer in front of us.

'But smart,' he persisted.

'We don't like it at school.'

He sat bolt upright as if someone had thumped him in the back. 'It doesn't matter whether you like it or not. It's smart.'

I said nothing and drank my tea. 'He's the one who has to wear it,' said my aunt mildly.

'And I'm the one who can judge the effect,' said my uncle. 'In Africa all my boys wore uniform; a fresh one every day. They used to starch the shorts. You could shave with the creases. It gave them self-respect. It helped the discipline.' What he was saying was new to me, but the rhythms were familiar. I knew without being told that he had delivered the same lecture many times before. It was like listening to Mr Gibbs on the subject of life in the trenches or Mr Sleath confessing his faith. Like a piece of music it had to run its course. The flow could not be interrupted. 'They had to pay for them out of their wages,' said my uncle. 'So much a week. And because of that they were proud of them. You could see your face in their buttons. They wore tarbooshes too, like little red flower-pots. Smart as paint, the lot of them. You can't tell me about uniform. I've seen how it works. Good for morale. Helps you to think straight.'

I watched the bees trundling through the heat haze and remembered the swish of serge at my ankles. Even the memory was stifling. 'I brought my gas-mask,' I said. 'The headmaster said we should take it everywhere we went.'

My uncle nodded approvingly. 'Sensible man.'

'He was in the trenches,' I said. 'In France. He's in the Territorials now.'

'Is he now?' said Uncle Frank. 'Well, it's all right for those with the opportunity.' He stood up abruptly and glowered at the garden as if in some way he had been challenged. He jingled the small change in his trouser pockets and cleared his throat. 'I'm going to take a bath,' he announced. 'We might go for a stroll later.'

I heard the water sing in the pipes as he turned the taps. 'Did I say something wrong?'

'Of course not.'

'But he seemed upset.'

My aunt patted my cheek. 'It wasn't your fault, he's just fussy about uniforms. Come and help me wash up.'

My uncle stayed in the bathroom for a long time and I told Aunt Edna about the school and how Sports Day had been spoiled by the sinking of the submarine and how my mother had been to see me earlier in the term with Mr and Mrs Aarons.

'Who did you say?'

'Mr and Mrs Aarons,' I said. 'They lived next door to Aunt Jenny. They've gone to America now.'

'And they were friends of your mother's?'

'Mrs Aarons was. Mr Aarons made her glasses.'

My aunt squeezed out the washing-up mop and untied her apron. 'And they've gone to America?'

'Mrs Aarons was worried about the war,' I said. 'She

thinks we're going to fight Germany and we'll be beaten. She offered to take me with her. Mother too. Sunshine and oranges. That's what she said.' My aunt looked puzzled. 'In California,' I explained. 'They grow them there.'

'And did you want to go?'

'I don't know. I wouldn't mind.'

Aunt Edna put her arm round my shoulders and led me into the living room. 'I don't think we should tell your Uncle Frank about this.'

'Why not?'

She hesitated. 'It might upset him. He might not understand.'

'About what?'

'About everything,' she said. 'You heard what he said about uniforms. He sees things one way and you see them differently. He didn't know your mother had a friend called Mrs Aarons. It's not one of his favourite names.'

'But she's very nice.'

'She's not one of us,' said my aunt. 'You know that don't you?'

'I know she's Jewish.'

'That's right,' said my aunt. 'She's Jewish and she's gone to America. Your uncle wouldn't think that was right.'

'He doesn't know her.'

'That's not the point,' said Aunt Edna. 'It's just something he feels and there's no sense in mentioning it if it's going to make him angry.' We heard the bath water gurgle down the waste pipe and my aunt put one red-tipped finger under my chin and tilted my head back. 'Nobody's telling you what you should think, but sometimes it's better not to argue. I can't bear people being cross about things that don't matter.'

'I won't tell him anything,' I said.

'That's the ticket.' She took a deep breath and pinched the waves in her hair more firmly into place. 'I think we both deserve a drink.' She gave me a fizzy lemonade and from an array of bottles on a side table tipped a measure of something brown and syrupy and something that looked like water into a jug half-filled with ice cubes. She stirred it with a long silver spoon and then poured it into a small tumbler.

She cut a sliver of peel from a lemon that lay beside the bottles and squeezed it over her glass. 'Heaven,' she said.

'What is it?'

Aunt Edna sipped her drink and showed me the tip of her tongue. 'It's a Martini.'

'Can I have a taste?'

'Just a little one.'

She held the glass to my lips and tilted it fractionally so that a few drops spilled into my mouth. 'It's like medicine,' I said.

'Medicine does you good.' She winked at me and took a much larger drink herself.

'Can I have some more?'

Aunt Edna looked sly. 'You're a bad boy. You'll get me into trouble.'

'No I won't, I promise.'

She gave me a small glass of my own and sprayed it with the lemon peel. 'Our secret,' she said, handing it to me. 'I won't tell your uncle and you mustn't tell your mother. You know what she thinks about people drinking.'

I remembered my mother's salute to temperance – 'Adam's grog!' – as she downed her tap water. 'I won't say anything.'

'It's not like telling lies,' said my aunt. 'It's what they call being discreet. You have to learn to respect people's feelings. You shouldn't upset them when there's no need to.'

'I understand.'

'I hope you do. It makes life so much easier.'

I thought how pretty she was perched on the arm of a chair, her legs crossed, the smoke from the cigarette she had just lit spinning through the sunlight that stretched like yellow planks from the window to the floor. I drained my glass and felt my head rock as if I had inhaled petrol. 'There are lots of things I don't tell my mother,' I said.

My aunt blew a perfect smoke ring. 'Perhaps you can tell me.'

'If you're interested.'

'Are they wicked things?'

I considered the list of possibilities. 'Some of them.'

'Such as?'

I heard my uncle coming down the passage. 'I'll tell you later,' I said.

'Don't forget.' Aunt Edna slid off her chair and met my uncle as he entered the room. She kissed him lightly on the mouth and handed him her glass. 'I've just had a little one. Why don't you mix us another?'

'Are you sure you've only had one?'

'One teensy-weensy little drink,' she said, measuring the amount between her fingers. 'Philip saw me. He'll tell you.'

'It was just one,' I said. 'I had a lemonade.'

Uncle Frank ignored me. 'The water's tepid,' he complained. 'It ran cold after a couple of minutes.'

'I'm sorry, darling. I'll get someone to see to the heater.'

'Tomorrow,' he said.

'Tomorrow, for sure.'

The drink seemed to cheer him up. He had several more and after dinner he suggested that we should take a walk on the front. He put on a striped blazer and a Panama hat and we strolled out into an evening that was sweet with the scent of lavender. Columns of midges danced over the fishpond, spiralling up and down like the bubbles in my lemonade. There was no breath of air until we reached the front and even there the only movement was a slight chill which brushed our cheeks as if we were walking beside a large plate glass window. I looked for breakers but all I could see was an expanse of glistening sand on which solitary men were digging for bait.

'Mother wanted me to watch the breakers coming in,' I said.

Uncle Frank looked seawards. 'What breakers?'

'Out there,' I said.

'We don't get breakers here,' said Aunt Edna. 'You can see how flat it is. You only get breakers where you have rocks and things.' Her explanation was vague, but I could see what she meant. I would have to be careful how I described it to my mother, I thought. I did not want to be blamed for a failure of the landscape.

'You know we asked your mother to come for a holiday,' said Uncle Frank. 'Several times, in fact.'

'She told me.'

'She needs to get out of that house. It's not good for her, looking at the same four walls every day.'

'She does get out sometimes,' I said. 'At least she did. She had a friend with a car who took her for drives.'

I felt Aunt Edna's warning nudge, but it was too late. I was not expecting to have to keep a secret so soon after I had been told what I should conceal. I did not even have time to invent an alias as I had done when Carpenter asked me the name of my mother's companion. I was overtaken by truth. 'Mrs Aarons,' I said.

My uncle stopped in mid-stride. 'Who did you say?'

'Mrs Aarons,' I said again. 'She lived next door to Aunt Jenny. She's gone to America.' I heard myself babbling as if I could disguise my initial blunder by covering it with more and more words. It was useless.

'Are you telling me,' said my uncle ominously, 'that your mother has a friend called Aarons?'

'Yes, she did. She's gone away now.'

'An Israelite?' he said. 'I don't believe you. No sister of mine would lower herself.'

His face was purple like the dusk that came striding in from the sea. He was angry with me but I sensed a greater rage building up behind his words which was directed not at any single person but against generations who he feared, of whom he knew nothing, but who he could blame for every disappointment in his own life. It was stupid, I thought. It was not fair that I had to defend Mrs Aarons. She was not even in England to defend herself. But as I listened to my uncle's tirade I knew the panic that she had felt when she described the arrests and the disappearance of her relatives in Germany.

'You'll see plenty of them down here,' said my uncle. 'Driving around in their flashy cars, stuffing themselves in the best hotels. They're trying to move in. And they've got the cash. Oodles of it. But you know what happens to a district when one of your friends buys himself a house? I'll tell you what happens. One of his cousins buys the house next door. And one of *his* cousins buys the house next door to *him*. And on and on until they own the whole bloody street.' He jabbed his finger in my chest. 'Then it's called a ghetto. And we're not wanted. We have to move out. But we're not going to let it happen. I can promise you that. We're going to stop them somehow.'

He was panting as if he had been running hard and he mopped his forehead with his handkerchief. Street lamps clicked on all along the front and I saw that he was sweating. My aunt took his elbow. 'Let's go home,' she said.

I turned my back on them. 'I don't want to come.'

'Suit yourself,' said my uncle. 'Go and find a nice Yiddisher momma.'

I wanted to hit him. I wanted never to see him again. I started to run towards Southend where the pier stuck its brilliant finger into the sea, but I knew that I would not be able to find my way back and after a while I slowed down and waited until my aunt came to collect me.

'You've done it now,' she said.

'I don't care. He's horrible.'

She cuffed the back of my head, not hard enough to hurt but to remind me that I was speaking out of turn. 'Don't be rude.'

'It's him who was rude.'

'He has his reasons for saying what he does.'

'They're stupid reasons.'

She jerked me to a halt and bent down to look into my face. 'That's enough,' she said sharply. 'If you're staying with me you're going to be polite.'

'It's him that's not polite.'

'He's upset. I told you he would be. You broke your promise.'

'I didn't mean to.'

'I know,' she said. 'But you must think before you speak.'

'I'm sorry.'

'It's your uncle you must say you're sorry to.'

'No,' I said. 'I won't do that.'

'You must,' said my aunt. 'You don't have to mean it. But you have to say the words. Otherwise you're going home, first thing.'

I apologised to my uncle the next morning and in the afternoon he went to London to stay at his club. When he came back a week later he said nothing about Mrs Aarons or the Israelites but the moment he stepped out of his car in the garage he flinched as if someone had brandished a fist in his face. 'What's that appalling smell?' he demanded.

I sniffed helpfully. 'I can't smell anything.'

'It's like dead fish,' he said.

I knew instantly what it was. The day he had gone to London my aunt had taken me out to buy the fishing tackle she had promised. We had also bought a can of lug worms to use as bait. After my initial enthusiasm had been cooled by two days of rain on Southend pier the lug worms had been abandoned in a corner of the garage where they now lay, wreathed in rainbow slime, rotting as the sun burned down from a cloudless sky. I buried them beneath the shrubbery, then went indoors and told Aunt Edna that I wanted to go home.

'But you were meant to stay for three weeks.'

I hung my head. 'I'm homesick. I want to see my mother.'

'It's not because of your uncle?'

'Not really.'

She looked doubtful for a moment, then tossed her head so that her hair sprang about her ears. 'We'll have to send a telegram,' she said. 'You can't just turn up out of the blue.'

'What will you say? I don't want to make any bother.'

'Can't we just tell her the truth?'

'It doesn't sound right,' I said. 'We'll have to think of something.'

'There's my own mother,' said Aunt Edna. 'I could always be called away to look after her.'

The telegram was despatched and two days later Uncle Frank drove me to London. Just before the train pulled out he pressed a pound note into my hand. 'Give your mother my love,' he said. 'There's no need to mention our disagreement.'

'I wasn't going to.'

'There's no point in upsetting her. It's no business of mine who her friends are.'

'All right,' I said. He was making an effort, I realised, but I could not respond as he wanted me to. I could still see his purple face the night we argued on the sea front and now it was confused with the lug worms choking in their own juices and I desperately wanted the train to be gone, bearing me through industrial estates and tunnels, by canals where anglers dreamed over their rods, over viaducts and meadows towards the heartland where arguments were understandable and the reasons for unhappiness were never disguised for long. I shook my uncle's hand and kissed my aunt goodbye and sat back in my corner seat so that I should not see them as the train left the station and I was removed from them as deftly as a letter dropped through the slot of a pillar box.

I told my mother I had missed her and gave both her and Mary boxes of chocolates and bags of sweets made to resemble sea shells. She hugged me and buried her nose in my hair. 'You smell of the sea,' she said. 'You're still salty.'

'I had a swim before breakfast.'

'I knew it,' she said triumphantly. 'Now tell me about the house.'

I thought hard. 'It was posh,' I began. 'They had this soft paper in the lav.'

'Fancy that,' said my mother.

'And we had orange juice for breakfast. From a tin. And we went for walks. And I went fishing.'

'Did you see the breakers?' she asked.

I did not hesitate. 'They were lovely,' I said. 'Like white horses. Like you said they'd be.'

I spent the rest of the holiday with the avenue gang playing in the marlpit and swimming in the open-air baths next to Smallthorne colliery where you could float on your back and watch the pit wheels turning against the summer sky. Once we walked to Knypersley where the mill pond was said to contain giant pike which devoured ducklings whole. And once I visited my father's grave in Burslem cemetery, close to the black marble obelisk erected to the memory of Arnold Bennett, and put fresh flowers in the vase sunk deep in the gravel chips.

There was a curious feeling of anticipation in the air which made us restless and on edge. My mother and Mary spent several days dusting and polishing the house as if we were expecting guests and Mr Gibbs sent a letter saying that in the event of an outbreak of hostilities my return to school might have to be postponed for two or three weeks while safety measures were brought up to the necessary standard.

'They've got to get new hose-pipes,' I said.

'It must be more than that.'

'And fire extinguishers. And black-out curtains.'

'You be careful who you tell about those things,' said my mother. 'It could be secret.'

We believed we were ready for the news, however bad it might be, but it was still a shock one Sunday morning when I went into the dining room to find my mother lying on the couch while from the radio behind her an old man's voice, as dry and punctilious as my Uncle Arthur's, told us that we were at war with Germany.

I reached for my mother's hand and held it tightly while enormous tears, like the pendants in her moonstone necklace, rolled down her face. I thought of Mrs Aarons safe in California and wished briefly that we were with her. 'Don't cry,' I said. 'I'll look after you. We'll be all right.'

She knocked my hand away as if it was a hot iron. 'I'm not crying for myself,' she said. 'Or for you. It's for those young men. So many are going to die.'

She stared out of the window, over the shed roof where the sparrows were pecking up the crumbs and I crept out of the room and wandered into the garden. I wondered if I should be crying myself and decided against it. Instead, I spread my arms and zoomed around the lawn spitting imaginary bullets at the lupins and the antirrhinums. No one stopped me. No one reminded me that it was Sunday and I should be quiet. I flew on wings of my own making into the first quiet morning of the war.